Fantastic Family Gatherings

Tried and True Ideas for Large and Small Family Reunions

by
Kathy Smith Anthenat

HERITAGE BOOKS, INC.

Published 1995 By

HERITAGE BOOKS, INC.
1540E Pointer Ridge Place, Bowie, MD 20716
(301) 390-7709

ISBN 0-7884-0229-3

A Complete Catalog Listing Hundreds of Titles
On History, Genealogy, and Americana
Available Free Upon Request

*To the Smiths, the Hindenburgs,
the Elliotts, the Anthenats, and the Ruples;
and to the wonderful patchwork quilt of memories
that all of them are creating for Alan and Kelly.*

Contents

V. Special Family Projects...123

VI. Recreation Ideas...137

   1. Balloon sweep relay
   2. Balloon pop relay
   3. Shoebox shuffle
   4. Crazy cane relay
   5. Balloon race relay
   6. Rolling relay
   7. Tricycle relay
   8. Egg in a tablespoon relay

   1. Lifesaver candy relay
   2. 'Necking'
   3. Bucket brigade
   4. Through the loop

   1. Stomp the balloon
   2. Water balloon battle
   3. Balloon shaving contest
   4. Balloon release

Recreation Ideas (Continued)

VII. A Closer Look at Four Reunions...169

VIII. State Tourism Offices...185

About This Book...

You probably are looking through this book because Aunt Jessica has just put you in charge of recreation for the next reunion. Or because you just attended one of those ho-hum-why-did-I-come reunions and you would like to help make the next one a gosh-that-was-fun-and-I-can't-wait-to-do-it-again event. Or because your family has never had a reunion and you think it sounds like a great idea. Or just because this book was sitting there on the shelf and looked like it might be interesting!

Whatever the reason, you have just opened up the most comprehensive book ever written about family reunions. Over four hundred families from across the United States were interviewed to find out how they organize their reunions, what activities work for them, and what they do to add sparkle and pizazz. Businesses which offer products of interest to family reunion organizers were contacted to find out what was available for imprinted mementos, record keeping supplies, etc. Brainstorming sessions resulted in helpful suggestions for everything from how to find a long lost relative to how to pay for the reunion. The result is this fabulous collection of tried and true ideas which have been organized into specific topics for easy reference.

Sometimes you read ideas in a how-to book and end up saying, "Sounds good in theory, but I don't think it would work in the real world." Many names have been included with the ideas in this book in order to stress that this book isn't just theory; real people have been using these ideas for their own very successful reunions. Try out a variety of the suggestions to find out what works best for your family. Next year try out some more!

At family reunions we can pick a fresh bouquet of memories that add a special fragrance to our lives. Enjoy that warm sense of belonging you feel when you arrive at the gathering spot and an uncle greets you with "I'm so glad you came!" Revel in listening to the older generation tell stories around the campfire of childhood pranks played on each other and their parents. Savor the taste of Grandma's special homemade peach cobbler in your mind as well as your mouth. Treasure the sight of a great aunt teaching your young daughter the old-fashioned art of tatting lace. Add to your bouquet those brief encounters of the friendly kind.

There is no one formula to use for a successful reunion. Have fun discovering the right ingredients to use for your very special and unique family. This book was written to help you consider all the wonderful possibilities.

Organizing the Reunion

THE BEGINNINGS OF A REUNION

There are all sorts of reasons why families decide to formally plan a reunion. Perhaps a family party is so enjoyable that everyone says, "Why don't we plan on doing this again?" Often the pursuit of careers has scattered a family so far geographically that the only way everyone can meet and catch up on each other's lives is to reserve a day on the calendar and plan on it. And sometimes people intent on researching their ancestors will organize a reunion so that all the family branches can meet and share information:

"Our Hamlett Reunion started out as a birthday dinner for my mother and father," says Dorothy Foster of Virginia. "Mom's birthday was October 7th, Dad's was September 26. So it usually fell in on the 4th Sunday in September. Daddy didn't like the fuss over him and some bringing presents, so he told everybody it would be just a get together. They had it every year on the same Sunday -- fourth Sunday in September. Word got around. Everybody came. Most would bring food, a folding chair, or even an old quilt. Some would bring a musical instrument -- guitar, autoharp, harmonica, etc. We would all have a grand time with kids playing together, trying to figure out whose kids are whose, sitting and reminiscing the good old days."

For the family of Brenda Gotensky of Michigan, yearly visits back to a childhood home evolved into an official reunion:

"Since we all were born in West Virginia and later moved away due to the coal mines shutting down, when we had children we wanted them to keep in touch with our family and friends back home," says Brenda. "So, yearly for the past twenty-odd years I would rent a cabin at a lodge/cabin area in the mountains near our town. Then everyone would make arrangements at the same time. After years of doing this my late cousin Linda said we should plan an official reunion the next year."

The Breen Reunion began in a graveyard. Five distant cousins (descendants of one of the original four Breen siblings who came to America in the mid 1800s) had been corresponding through the mail, sharing genealogical information. They finally decided to meet at a cemetery where some of their ancestors are buried:

"We spent the day getting acquainted and sharing information, had lunch at a nearby restaurant, and looked up a couple of other cousins living in the area," says Mary Henson of Alabama. "By the next year we contacted more relatives; some were descendants of other siblings. The following year was the year we really organized. We elected officers, decided to start a newsletter, and voted to have the next reunion in two years -- which we did with sixty-three persons there from nine states and one foreign country."

If you would like to organize a reunion for your family, start by making a few phone calls or writing a few letters to see if anyone else is interested in a gathering of the clan. The following is an example of a letter which could be used for this purpose:

Dear Cousin Fred,

Several of us have been talking about holding a reunion for all of us Hendersons next June at the Flora Park. It would be great to see everyone together and our children would have an opportunity to get acquainted with their cousins.

Aunt Margaret and Cousin David are excited about the idea. How about you? Could you reserve June 13 on your calendar and join us at the park for the afternoon?

Your cousin,
Kathy Henderson

Depending on the size and type of reunion you have in mind, you may want to send out questionnaires with a cover letter to find out what type of reunion others are interested in. Possible questions to include are: Any suggestions for when and where to hold the reunion? What kind of family reunion would you be interested in -- picnic, formal dinner, backyard cookout, etc.? How long? How many from your family would be attending? What type of lodging would be needed (campgrounds, motel, relatives' homes)? Any thoughts on how we should handle expenses?

Specify a date by which you would like a reply. Ask them to spread the word about the plans for a reunion, and also to send to you the addresses of anyone else who ought to be included on the mailing list for information about it.

SHARING THE WORK AND THE DECISIONS

Even for the simplest and most common type of family reunion -- a bring-a-dish lunch at a local park -- someone has to make some decisions and do some work. Someone has to set a date and time, let everyone know about it, reserve a rainshelter in case of rain, supply place settings and drinks, say a few words to welcome everyone, decide on and arrange any planned activities, and clean up the area afterwards. There is one big advantage to sharing this work: usually, the more people you involve in putting together an event the greater the number of people who will likely show up for it.

In some families there is a host family or group for each reunion and they take care of all responsibilities and decisions:

"My mother is one of eleven children and from the time their father died in 1939 they have taken turns hosting a reunion -- from the oldest child to the youngest child, every year on the first Saturday in August," says Mary Garbutt of Idaho. "The oldest daughter is dead, but her two children live in close proximity so they have decided to together take their mother's turn in line. The children of the host have cleanup duty, making sure everyone takes home their empty dishes, and tossing out all the paper plates, etc."

In another family a particular generation has the responsibility of putting together the reunions. The generation that began the annual reunions has now passed the responsibility for organizing them down to the next generation. Each family in that generation is assessed a small amount to pay for postage, phone calls, etc.

In the Bland family a local host sponsors the gathering and the reunion that year is dedicated to the hosts' historical family. Previous hosts present a 'hosts' plaque to the new one; the plaque includes the name and city of the host (and all past hosts) and is his or hers to display for one year.

Many families nominate committees to handle all of the reunion details. The Coburn Reunion has a nominating committee composed of family members who are seventy-plus years old:

"We even have a special name for them -- 'The Originals'," says family member Jo Ann Casebier of Kansas. "It was this generation that originally started the reunion, hence the name. Committees are selected at one reunion to be responsible for the next reunion; sometimes the planning is well underway before the current reunion is over since the committee members may live in different states. No two members of the same family serve on the same committee except for church services and search committee, which is done by couples."

Sometimes families elect reunion officers at one reunion and these officers are responsible for forming any committees they need to help them put together the next reunion. A variety of names could be used for these officers, depending on how you want to divide up the work to be done, but the most common are:
1. President - presides at meetings and guides the group as to what style of reunion will be planned for the coming year
2. Vice President - presides when the president is unavailable; often becomes the next president
3. Treasurer - keeps records of all money and pays all bills
4. Secretary - takes notes at all meetings and sends out all notices
5. Historian - keeps records of all births, deaths, marriages, etc. in the family, often in a reunion scrapbook

Committees could be used in any of the following areas instead of or in addition to the officers: program, recreation, food, lodging, welcoming, hospitality, registration, decorating, transportation, photography, cleanup, publicity, and communication.

The officers/committees meet as often as necessary to discuss plans and make decisions. If you have committees let them do their work and let them get started on it as soon as possible. Try to avoid overloading any one person. Keep in mind though that the work for most reunions is carried out by a small group of people who are dedicated to continuing the reunions.

No matter how well activities, food quantities, and other details are planned there are bound to be some problems. Be flexible. Start early and reconfirm everything twice, and then again.

It is best to keep your first reunion very simple and flexible, such as a potluck picnic at a park with a pavilion. A few unexpected arrivals or dropouts won't affect the party that much. Don't overplan the event and don't forget to enjoy the day yourself!

WHEN? HOW LONG? HOW OFTEN?

Large reunions are usually held during the summer months for several reasons: the weather is pleasant so that all or part of the reunion activities can be held outdoors where there is more room to spread out, school-age children aren't in school, and families who will need to travel a long distance to attend can make it part of their family vacation. Long weekends such as Memorial Day, the Fourth of July, and Labor Day are popular for reunions because adults can get away from work. The most popular month is June (especially for families who camp outdoors during the reunion) because the weather is the most temperate that month -- not too hot and not too cold -- and outdoor bugs are usually less of a problem then than they will be later in the summer.

There are some advantages to holding reunions during other times of year. Meeting at a popular resort during the off-season can be a lot less expensive. One family chooses New Year's Day because the families involved are too busy with their own schedules during the summer.

"On my father's side the reunion is always on New Year's Day," says Mary Garbutt of Idaho. "Whomever 'feels the need' hosts an open house January 1. Everyone brings all their leftover Christmas goodies. There is always a TV room for football and a separate room for gabbing. Some people stay all day and some come and go. Sometimes somebody will say 'my place next year' but usually nobody does until just before Christmas and then whoever starts calling around first is the hostess. Sometimes it just doesn't happen but then we all miss it so much it doesn't often get missed two years in a row. There's been talk lately to make it in the summer but everybody seems to have conflicting schedules. New Year's Day seems to be a kind of slack off and sit-around time for everybody, so it works for us."

Set the date for your reunion as early as possible so that people can coordinate their vacations around it. Many families have a standing date, such as the second full weekend in June, so that there is never a question about which weekend the family reunion is. Remember, chances are that no date is going to be ideal for everyone. Once the date is set, stick with it.

Lengths of reunions vary from a couple of hours to ten days and are held anywhere from twice a year to once every five years. The Coburn reunion is held every three years and meets from Friday afternoon to Monday morning. The Fry(e) reunion in Ohio is held one day annually, lasting six to eight hours. The National Fry(e) Reunion is held every two years for two days, four hours each day. Another family group meets for one weekend every four years; to make it easy to keep track of which year is a reunion year they hold it on presidential election years.

WHERE?

Once you decide when to have the reunion and how long to have it you need to find a location. Small gatherings can be held at a family member's house; many families prefer that type of warm, loving atmosphere. A rented tent can be set up in the backyard for extra space, shade, and rain protection.

When Jan Burkart hosted a family gathering at her home in Minnesota, half of the reunion fun took place on a bus! She is the oldest of seven children and Christmas has always been a family time for her. For twenty-six years she, her husband, and children drove back to the hometown in Wisconsin in order to join the rest of the family for the Christmas holidays. When the family got too big for her mother's apartment she suggested rotating the gatherings at the siblings' homes. Jan offered to begin at her place, but it was in Minnesota and the rest of the family was in Wisconsin. One of her brothers, a coach driver, solved the problem by driving the thirty-five family members to Jan's home in a chartered coach! When they arrived the family sang songs, ate family favorite foods, played games, told childhood stories, and enjoyed each other's company for two days. Sleeping arrangements included sofas, beds, cots, sleeping bags, and a few rooms at a local hotel. Jan says that her only regret is that she didn't get to participate in all the fun during the bus trip itself to and from her home!

For some families holding a reunion in a private home can be very stressful; rambunctious small children can accidentally break items or get into something dangerous at a home that has not been childproofed. Holding the reunion on neutral ground at a park or hotel prevents anyone from feeling like they have to entertain everyone else.

Reserve the location for your reunion early: "When our reunion is over the first thing we do is reserve the location for the next year," says Sonia Cesarino of Pennsylvania. "We pay the rent for the pavilion for the next year the day of our reunion."

Keep in mind when choosing a location that there is no guarantee what the weather will be like on the chosen day; be prepared for inclement weather. Here are some other things to consider:
1. Are the restrooms within a reasonable distance and in working order? (Portable outhouses can be rented for outdoor locations.)
2. Is there handicap access, if needed?
3. Is there adequate parking?
4. Is it a safe place for children? Is there an area where they can play?
5. Is there plenty of seating available?
6. Is the location reasonably accessible to the whole family? (Elderly members of the family may not be physically able to travel very far.)
7. Make sure the place is neither too large nor too small for your family's needs.
8. If the reunion will last more than two days, are there plenty of activities to enjoy within easy driving distance?

Check with your local Chamber of Commerce or Department of Tourism Development for possible reunion sites. Perhaps an area church, government agency, or other organization has a conference center which will fit your needs. The Allison Family Reunion in Indiana uses either a 4-H building or the fellowship hall of a church. The Cathey Reunion Association reunions are also held at a church:

"Following church service on Sunday we have registration and food," says Mary Cathey Summers of North Carolina. "Everyone brings a picnic filled basket and we furnish paper plates, napkins, cups, eating utensils, iced tea, and lemonade."

The Pinkston Reunion in Dorchester, Illinois is held at the Village Hall: "It includes heat and air conditioning," says Freida Price, "and we are fortunate to be able to rent it for $25."

Ruth Brown of Indiana reports that the Boehm Family Reunion was held in the old schoolhouse one year "...so that everyone could feel closer and be more familiar with it when the older relatives talked about the school." The Minnich Family Reunion, which included 249 people from sixteen states, was held in the school cafeteria in Philo, Ohio:

"We paid for the school house and a janitor," says Virginia Minnich. "We had a kitchen, water, refrigerator, and ice maker."

The Skidmore and Dawson Family Reunion was held at a Salvation Army gymnasium, and the Harris Reunion was held at a Senior Citizens Community Building in Wamego, Kansas:

"We used to hold this (Harris) reunion in the park rather than the air conditioned building," says Jo Ann Casebier, "and started losing our crowd as the older family members wanted to be in a comfortable place to eat and not fight bugs. They also wanted to assure that we didn't have to worry if it was too hot, rainy, etc."

The Himes-Shaffer Family Reunion is held at a local 4-H Center: "It is private and has plenty of parking space," says Roberta Mingyar of West Virginia. "The building is air conditioned with a kitchen and toilet facilities." It is located on one level -- a big plus for the elderly and the very young."

The Fred and Beaulah Hamrick Reunion is also held at a 4-H facility: "We like it because it has lots of space inside, a kitchen, and restrooms," says JoAnne McIntyre of West Virginia. "It has a large grassy area where children can play games and not get hurt. There is air conditioning inside and it is especially nice in the evening because we have a live band that comes about 8 P.M. and we dance until midnight. It is the highlight of the day!"

National, state, county, and city parks are popular sites for reunions. You will need to reserve campsites, cabins, rain shelters, or whatever is needed well in advance. One member of the family should inspect each proposed site before a final selection is made.

"We rented a building at a city park at a very reasonable rate," says Carol Wilson of Wisconsin. "We needed a building to show slides, give awards, and in case of inclement weather. There were outdoor roofed pavilions for meals. Be sure to ask about other events taking place nearby."

The Sarine-Sirrine-Surine Reunion was held at a state park: "We reserved a pavilion near the entrance," says Carolyn Surine of New York. "As it turned out, it was cool and rainy so we had fires in both fireplaces and were able to set up under cover."

In some parks you can't reserve a rain shelter; it's strictly "first-come, first-served." Members of the Lamb Reunion came up with a solution to this problem:

"A new tradition is a pancake breakfast early in the morning at the park shelter house," says George Carlisle of Illinois. "Since one has to get there early anyway to reserve it for the group we decided that pancakes would be fine for those from a distance."

The Lamb Family used a group camp one year at Sequoia State Park near Waggoner, Oklahoma that consisted of ten A-frame cabins with bunk beds (users must furnish their own bedding). One cabin had a private bath and the others used a bath house. The cost of $125 per day included a large dining hall and a picnic shelter. There were also tennis courts, golf, and swimming available at the park; boats, including pontoon boats for up to a dozen, were available for about $75 per day.

Imagine how much fun it could be to house your whole gathering in one dormitory for the reunion. Lake Fort Smith State Park (P.O. Box 4, Mountainburg, AR 72946, 501-369-2469 or 800-264-2435) has a group dormitory with a kitchen and hall available for rent; the cost for 31 to 110 people is $5 per person per day, with an additional charge of $35 per day for the use of the kitchen. Family members can rent a canoe for $15 per day, play tennis, go hiking on the trails, relax, and visit.

One note about outdoor, overnight reunions: even if the majority of the people attending the reunion want to camp out, make sure there are also motels near the campsite for those who do not enjoy camping.

Summer camps and college dormitories (during their off seasons) are other alternatives. Some of these places furnish all the food; at others you can use the kitchen facilities there to do your own cooking.

The Cooper Reunion was held at Calvin College in Grand Rapids, Michigan, lasting from Thursday afternoon to Saturday afternoon. Ruth Cooper Bouma of Texas describes the very relaxing and enjoyable reunion: "We hired babysitters from the college job service and paid them out of the general fund. We asked the visual arts department on campus to set us up with a large color TV and VCR in a comfortable room with lots of seating for the children and we played movies for them at scheduled times. We planned lots of outdoor activities for older children. Also swimming. We took in an organ concert that was scheduled on campus during our stay and reserved time at the science building observatory in the late evening to look at the stars as well as the Fourth of July fireworks nearby. The dorms have lovely furnished basements with easy chairs, a lot of tables, a large television room for the children, ping-pong and pool tables, table hockey, etc. The kids had a ball. Some people brought their bikes and used them and skateboards to good advantage. The food service bent over backwards to give us excellent food, plenty of it, right on time, and even a soft ice cream machine, unlimited seconds, and they didn't hurry us out of the building either. We were allowed to sit and talk over coffee for as long as we liked."

The National Robinett Reunion is held at the campus of Westminster College in Fulton, Missouri. Ancestors Allen and Margaret Robinett were married there in the Church of St. Mary in 1653.

Some families hold reunions in the same location each year while others prefer variety:

"One year we had a hog roast and campfire ceremony at the Carlisle farm," says George Carlisle of Illinois. "In 1988 the reunion was held at a Winter Park, Colorado resort, hosted by family members who operate a raft float trip and ski livery service. We had a raft trip down the Colorado River, jeep rides up mountains, and condominiums for each family and a central dining hall where we brought food for community meals and had our game and church service sessions. In 1990 we had a group camp at Fort Gibson Lake near Tahliquah, Oklahoma. The hosting family members rented a pontoon boat to go around the lake. In 1991 we were at "The Landing" resort near Hannibal, Missouri, a water park with cabins. This park had small housekeeping cabins where we could cook our food and bring it up to a central shelter to eat together. We took advantage of the wave pool, water slides, etc."

The Seeley Genealogical Society changes locations to make the gatherings accessible to more people. Past reunions have been in Colorado, Indiana, and Connecticut. Future reunions are planned in Salt Lake City and Canada.

The John and Elizabeth Curtis/Curtiss Society gatherings are usually held in Connecticut, but they are going to try holding the reunions in other areas where there is a cluster of members:

"A family branch in Michigan offered to host the 1993 reunion, so we are going to try it," says Barbara Curtis Weaver, president of the society. "If it is successful we will hold the reunion in Connecticut one year and elsewhere the next."

The idea of alternating locations might also be a good compromise in a family where part of the members prefer a resort-type reunion and part prefer camping out. Alternate styles; hold an elegant reunion at a lavish resort one year and a back-to-basics camp-out in a forest preserve the next.

Nothing creates lasting memories quite like a shared adventure, so consider one for your gathering. How about a trek through the Grand Canyon, an old-fashioned wagon train journey, or a canoe trip? One good book to consult for location possibilities is *Super Family Vacations: Resort and Adventure Guide*, by Martha Shirk and Nancy Klepper (New York: Harper Perennial, 1992). It lists locations suitable for family vacations and describes the accommodations, dining, activities for children, special niceties of the place, and how to get more information.

Dude ranches are popular for week-long family gatherings. Larry and Cheryl Erickson of California held their reunion at the Scott Valley Resort and Guest Ranch (P.O. Box 1447 FFG, Mountain Home, AR 72653, tel. 501-425-5136). They suggest holding a reunion at a place that offers pre-arranged activities for all ages so that one person doesn't have to be the social director. The Scott Ranch fit the bill with horseback riding, pool, tennis, volleyball, shuffleboard, cookouts, hayrides, ferry tours, etc. Nearby attractions include trout fishing, canoeing, scuba diving, sailing, and golf.

The owner of the ranch, Kathleen Cooper, says they get a lot of family reunions because "this is one of those places where everyone has a good time! No one person gets stuck cooking, cleaning, and thinking up things to keep everyone happy!"

The owner of the Quarter Circle U Rankin Ranch (P.O. Box 36-FR, Caliente, CA 93518, tel. 805-867-2511), Helen Rankin, has also noticed an increase of family reunions at her ranch over the last few years:

"With the hectic pace of life in the city we know our guests enjoy letting us do the planning for these family gatherings," says Helen. "We can accommodate up to forty people with our twelve rooms and when a group takes the entire accommodations we are happy to plan all the activities to their specifications. It's a perfect vacation for all ages and especially for families."

The Rankin Ranch offers a peaceful atmosphere and plenty of activities: horseback riding, swimming, tennis, hay-wagon rides, barbecues, fishing, hiking, volleyball, shuffleboard, square dances, bingo, pool tournaments, talent shows, and even horse races with prizes for the winners. The children's activity director coordinates swim meets, nature hikes, scavenger hunts, and arts and crafts, and the children can even help feed the baby animals.

Mr. and Mrs. Abraham Luboff of California chose this ranch for a gathering of twenty-nine family members and friends to celebrate their 50th wedding anniversary. They thoroughly enjoyed the horseback riding, the delicious food, and relaxing atmosphere:

"There was time to spend with little ones and time for adults, some of whom we had not seen for quite a while and others with whom we had almost daily contact but all being much too busy for intimate contact," says Abraham. "On the evening before we departed they had prepared a hayride and a barbecue out in a meadow. It was the most delicious barbecue I had ever tasted."

Hotels and resorts with meeting and banquet rooms are a natural for large national reunions and an increasing number of them are wooing families with group discounts, complimentary meeting rooms, and other enticements. Ask if the banquet room is free with a certain number of room bookings.

Ideally you will be able to find a resort with a wide range of accommodations, such as double rooms, family rooms, and cottages (with or without kitchens) which accommodate varying numbers of people. Mixing up the generations for lodging can be a wonderful experience -- sharing togetherness and fun.

Check to see if there are adequate parking facilities for cars and RVs; take notice especially of any low entry overhead clearances in parking garages that will prevent RVs from entering. Some hotels will allow RVs to park free on hotel grounds with persons staying in them, assuming that they will still be picking up revenue from meals bought there with the rest of the reunion attendees.

Include the following in a signed contract with a hotel: firm dates, room rates and taxes, meeting facility description (and cost if any), and the cost of catered luncheon and banquet dinner with a set menu (get prices per person including tax and gratuity). Stanton Rickey of the Rickey Family Association suggests that you be sure that the hotel understands that you do not want 'auditorium seating' or even 'banquet seating' if the gathering is for genealogical research purposes:

"We need room to spread out charts, maps, albums, etc.; therefore typical banquet tables that seat ten for meals should only accommodate four or six people intent on genealogy," says Stanton. "Have peripheral tables for photocopiers, computers, displays, etc. Have the hotel provide a U.S. flag, piano, raised platform or stage, podium and small adjacent table, easels, microphone, and speakers. Get permission to staple or tape banners, flags, maps, etc. to the walls."

Wilma Cullison of Indiana has the following comments concerning her experiences with lodging for the Fithian Family Reunion: "The most frustrating problem I had was with one motel. We asked for a block of rooms to be set aside and whenever someone called for reservations they were told there were none available. It was easier for people to call me and then I went to the motel and made reservations. Also, there were late parties with loud music and dancing that kept several awake. If I were doing this again I would ask persons to make reservations through me. I would specify ground level rooms (we had some 90 years old on walkers) and away from party area."

David Dray, the general manager of Holiday Inn Southeast in Chattanooga, Tennessee recommends that you have the following information ready before discussing arrangements with a hotel:
1. The approximate number of rooms needed to house your reunion.
2. Food requirements, private dining, children's meals, who pays for group functions, etc.
3. Transportation needs to the airport or even to attractions, malls, etc.
4. Ask about children's activities, game room, pool, etc.

He suggests that some extras to look for from a potential hotel for your reunion are:
1. A flat room rate for one to four people
2. A complimentary room for every twenty booked -- to be used at the planner's discretion
3. A complimentary hospitality room
4. Reservation cards to send to the family members
5. A welcome message on the hotel marquee
6. The availability of packages which include T-shirts, banners, etc.
7. Possible discount tickets to area attractions

"A hotel can be used in two ways," says David. "One would be only for housing overnight guests and the other would be as the headquarters or center of activity, provided that they have the facilities that are needed for a particular family reunion."

LETTING EVERYONE KNOW ABOUT THE REUNION

Getting the word out about a backyard family gathering could be as simple as a few local phone calls. A large national reunion for a particular surname could involve months of searching for addresses of people who would be interested, three or four rounds of notices and registration forms, etc. This section contains a variety of ideas from which you can pick what is appropriate for your situation.

The first thing to decide is: Who is invited? Is the reunion for one set of grandparents and all their descendants (including spouses)? Is it for all descendants of a specific immigrant ancestor who was the first in the family to come to America? Is it open to anyone with a particular surname or who has descended from someone with that surname? Will long-time friends of the family be invited?

Sonia Cesarino, a member of the Bock Reunion says, "We always enjoy when guests and our relatives have other relatives attend and they are always welcome. Some friends have attended more reunions than some relatives! We send out notices to two local newspapers and to the local radio station's bulletin board. We sent in a notice to Everton's *Genealogical Helper* mainly because we were hoping to find other Bock family researchers."

If the reunion will be fairly large with the attendees spread out geographically you will need a mailing list with addresses of everyone who should be notified. A computer will make the task of compiling and updating such a list much simpler. If you don't have one ask around to see if someone else in the family who does would be willing to help out.

"I spent the greater part of a year attempting to make contact with families I hoped would turn out to be descendants of immigrant Heinrich Frey and invited them to attend our national reunion in the event that they had any knowledge at all of being descended from this person," says Bert Frye of Ohio. "In my letters I enclosed a blank paternal ancestry chart to be filled in by those who were interested. From this I did a computer generated flow chart network of family lineages from our immigrant ancestor, which I displayed at the reunion. This seemed to be of interest to all who attended." He found that personal notes were more effective than formal invitations, and that the organizer must have plenty of patience and tenacity and be willing to devote many hours prior to the reunion event in corresponding with prospective attendees.

Figure 1. An example of an informal letter about an upcoming reunion. Certain phrases are highlighted with bold lettering for easy skimming of the information included.

REUNION NEWSLETTER

Dear Williamson Kith and Kin,

Plans are being made for the **1994 Williamson Family Reunion**. Mark your calendars now for fabulous food, fun and catching up!!

It will be held **June 22 at the Wane County Preserve enclosed shelter**. The doors open at **10:00**. There will be a "WE HAVE ARRIVED!" tree at the welcoming table; be sure to hang your heart on the tree. We have extra hearts for friends and newcomers, so let's have that tree loaded with hearts of friendship and love by the end of the day! We also have a packet of souvenirs and goodies for each family.

Lunch will be served at 12:30. The reunion committee will supply ham and chicken. Please bring a casserole or salad, and a dessert to share. Grandma Dora says she will be bringing her famous Glorified Rice again and Uncle Victor will be making plenty of Hungry Cookies; I can taste them already! Bring your own silverware, plates, & cups. Iced tea, lemonade, milk, orange juice, and coffee will be supplied; if you want something else feel free to bring it, but no alcoholic beverages.

All you cooks get ready for the **Third Annual Chili Contest** in the evening. Trophies will be awarded and we all get to eat the contest entries for supper! There will also be a campfire to roast weinies and marshmallows on.

Cousin Anne won't tell me what **activities and games** she has planned but she gets this big grin on her face every time I ask her how the plans are coming along! She suggests bringing a change of clothing for all children, because they're probably going to get wet!

Don't forget about our **annual craft auction**! For newcommers to our reunion, we hold an auction at 3:00 p.m. each year to cover expenses for the next year. Use your talents to create something special for the auction table: wall hangings, embroidery, lap robe, carvings, homemade note paper, framed poem about the family, Christmas tree ornament, etc. Half the fun is seeing what everyone else decided to make!

We all turn to pumpkins at 10:00 (have to be out of the shelter), so we need to start cleaning up at 9:00 p.m.

If you have any suggestions or comments, please let any of us on the reunion committee know.

Meg Williamson   Vickie Harms
Karen Jones   Jennifer Williamson

Figure 2. Another type of reunion notice. Be sure to include a phone number.

!WANTED!

All Descendants of
JOEL AND ANGELINE CROGAN

LAST SEEN
not too long ago; last year;
when they were knee-high to a grasshopper; too long ago

VITAL STATISTICS
Size ranges from tiny twigs to sturdy branches.
Members of a strong, growing family tree with deep roots.
Much loved.

URGENT!
If you have seen or know the whereabouts
of any of these descendants,
please notify them immediately that their presence
is requested at the

1994 CROGAN FAMILY REUNION

August 24, 1994 * 11:00 a.m. to 4:00 p.m.

At the home of Jim and Martha Crogan

16645 Meadowbrook Avenue, Anytown, ND

Phone 423-9888 to report any sightings, acceptances, or regrets.

One family uses 'contact people' to broadcast the information about upcoming reunions:

"I have one contact person per family," explains Diane Brown of Alabama. "When I write the letter announcing the reunion, follow-up letters, etc., I only have to send one to the contact person. They are responsible for letting their families know the information. All the family members know who their contact person is so they ask them periodically for information. This really saves postage and keeps communication open within the families. The person must be responsible and interested in continuing the reunions."

If you are looking for others who might want to attend the reunion (especially if it is at least partially being held for the purposes of furthering genealogical research) you might want to send a notice of the event to Everton's *Genealogical Helper*, a magazine published every other month that includes a section called 'Upcoming Genealogical Events'. As space permits (free of charge) notices of special genealogical events (including family reunions) are published in this section. The details must be received four months before the date of the event; include the name of the group holding the event, the date, the place, brief details about the event, and a name, address, and telephone number for a contact person. Send entries to 'Upcoming Genealogical Events', The Everton Publishers, Inc., P.O. Box 368, Logan, Utah 84321. This magazine also has a section -- 'Missing Folk Finder' -- where you can place ads to try to locate missing relatives.

Another magazine possibility for getting the attention of others who might want to attend your reunion is *Reunions* magazine. There is no charge for listing your family reunion in the *Reunions* Family RegisTREE. Use the form in the magazine or just send the name of the family reunion, contact person, address, phone number, FAX, date and place of the reunion, and how many you expect to attend to *Reunions* Family RegisTREE, P.O. Box 11727, Milwaukee, WI 53211-0727. Distinguish your family by explaining how they are related -- from whom they all descend. Anyone wishing to search for a family reunion can send a self-addressed stamped envelope with the request to the magazine. (This magazine also contains a directory of reunion-friendly facilities, listed by state and city.)

There are several directories available which will include a listing for your family reunion free of charge in the next updated edition of their publication. Be sure to include the name and address of a contact person for your reunion. When browsing through these directories you may discover another reunion that you would like to participate in!

1. *Directory of Family Associations*, compiled by Elizabeth Petty Bentley (Genealogical Publishing Co., 1001 North Calvert Street, Baltimore, MD 21202). Lists family associations, reunion committees, one name societies, surname exchanges, and family newsletters.

2. *Family Associations, Societies, and Reunions*, edited by J. Konrad (Summit Publications, P.O. Box 222, Munroe Falls, OH 44262). Lists family associations and reunions in the U.S. and Canada.

3. *Family Periodicals and Reunions*, compiled by Mrs. Merle Ganier (2108 Grace Street, Ft. Worth, TX 76111).

If you have lost touch with some family members over the years and would like to mail them an invitation to the reunion -- but can't find their current address -- here are some possibilities for locating them:

1. The Social Security Administration has a letter forwarding service that might help you contact a lost loved one if it is a matter of great importance of which he or she is unaware and about which he or she would undoubtedly want to be informed. There is no charge for forwarding a letter which has a humanitarian purpose, such as a serious illness or death in the immediate family. The Social Security Administration reads each letter to ensure that it contains nothing which could be embarrassing to the missing person if read by a third person. Send the letter in a plain, unstamped, unsealed envelope showing only the missing person's name to the Office of Public Inquiries, Social Security Administration, 6401 Security Boulevard, Baltimore, MD 21235. Be sure to supply identifying information such as the person's social security number or the person's date and place of birth, father's name, and mother's full maiden name.

2. Find People Fast (TM) is a computerized information service that provides assistance in locating adults living in the U.S. If there is no match for the information you are requesting there is no charge. Contact them at: Find People Fast, Infomax, Inc., 4600 Chippewa, Suite 244, St. Louis, MO 63116, tel. (314) 481-3000 or toll free (800) 829-1807, FAX (314) 832-0029.

3. *How to Locate Anyone Anywhere Without Leaving Home*, by Ted L. Gunderson (New York: E.P. Dutton, 1989) is a excellent book for ideas on how to locate missing people.

4. Computer bulletin boards, such as Prodigy, can also be helpful to both spread the word about your reunion (place a note on the Genealogy or Reunions sections) and find missing people (place a notice in the Missing section and ask other Prodigy members -- who are extremely helpful -- to check their phone books for a person by that name).

Inform people of the date and general location of the reunion as soon as possible; a year in advance is ideal for large reunions. You can follow up with more complete information later. This may include:

1. a recommendation of casual or formal attire
2. date, hours, place
3. the location of the nearest airport, train station, bus station
4. number for a car rental agency
5. numbers, addresses, and general rates for hotels, motels, campgrounds
6. interesting attractions and events in the area for those families who will be attending as part of their planned vacation
7. map and directions
8. a request for their participation in a sharing table, picture display, auction, talent show, etc.; recipes for a recipe book or any memory makers you've chosen
9. ask if anyone has any special needs, such as wheelchair accessibility or a no-salt diet
11. make special policies about bringing guests or pets
12. ask for volunteers to bring certain items or to take care of certain duties

The publicity chairman, if you have one, should be in charge of preparing and sending out news releases to appropriate magazines, genealogy society newsletters, and local newspapers. Check in advance to see what form the notice or article about your reunion should be submitted in, and how early it should be submitted. All articles should be typed, double-spaced, on one side of 8 1/2" x 11" paper. Be sure to mention the date you would like the announcement to appear.

One final note from Mary Cathey Summers of North Carolina about invitations to a reunion: "I would like to emphasize that we do not send out invitations, as some would say 'I didn't go because I did not get an invitation'; so, we send out notices."

EXPENSES

There are a variety of ways to deal with the costs involved in organizing and holding a family reunion. A hat is passed for voluntary contributions at the Elliott Reunion. The expenses of the Kelly Reunion are taken care of by the six brothers and sisters. The McEwen Dawson Family Reunion organizers request a donation of $20 per family:

"Another way we raise money is with our musical," says family member Martha Grubbs of Kentucky. The family chooses a church to perform a musical in and takes up a collection afterwards.

Marie Boeder-Bartholomay of North Dakota reports: "We charged $3.00 per family service charge and then charged for each member; as an adult they paid for the adult meal and then 5-10 we charged a junior fee. Some people donated money and some of the money left over on the souvenirs was used."

Many families hold family auctions to raise money to finance their reunions (see Chapter IV Fundraising Ideas). Sometimes family members will donate money which is specifically earmarked for a certain expense:

"One aunt always donates the money for us to buy the hamburgers, hot dogs, and other meats with," says Sonia Cesarino of Pennsylvania. This family also holds a family auction, a 50-50 raffle, and other events to raise money for the reunion fund.

Sometimes the grandparents will pay the entire cost to take all of their descendants to somewhere special such as a dude ranch, where they can enjoy each other's company away from the daily details of life at home. Mr. and Mrs. Roy Reiman pick up the tab for a common vacation/reunion for their six children and spouses and the grandchildren -- now spread out in six states:

"We pick a different vacation spot for this reunion each time, and my wife and I pick up the entire tab," says Roy, the editor/publisher of *Country* magazine. "We tell the kids it's their 'will money' we're spending -- that we're spending it with them instead of leaving it for them." The gathering is scheduled each year during the week of their anniversary and the children are told not to buy any gifts; their presence at the gathering is the only gift the Reimans want.

Another grandfather chooses to finance a family reunion at a nice resort in lieu of individual birthday and Christmas presents for the children and grandchildren. The family whole-heartedly supports this exchange. "That week together is something we all look forward to all year," says one son. "Dad always chooses a resort with plenty of activities that we all can do, especially things he and Mom can do with their grandchildren. They're making precious memories that no birthday or Christmas present could match."

If you will be charging a per-person fee for a reunion which covers a banquet dinner, lodging, etc., request that families pay at least half the amount within thirty days from the receipt of the letter, with the other half due ninety days before the reunion. This will assure working capital and give you an idea of how many to expect.

Be cost-conscious in setting the amount to be borne by each person or family. "Too many families are pricing their reunions far out of reach of less affluent members of the family. That is the way to keep them from coming, if that is the goal, but what kind of decent family would do that?" comments one person who is upset with this trend.

Figure 3. Sample reservation/order form for more elaborate reunions.

Reservation/Order Form for
1994 McLAUGHLIN FAMILY REUNION

1. August 13 (Lunch)

    Number of people attending ____ x $8.00 per person $_____

2. August 14 (Picnic)

    Number of people attending ____ x $8.25 per person $_____

3. August 15 (Buffet Dinner and Dance)

    Number of people attending ____ x $33.75 per person $_____

4. All three events/days including meals, activities, etc.

    Number of people attending ____ x $50.00 per person $_____

SUBTOTAL $_____

5. T-Shirts

    Kids Size 6-8 ($4.85 each) x _____(number required) $_____

    Adult small ($5.25 each) x ____ (number required) $_____

    Adult medium ($5.25 each) x ____ (number required) $_____

    Adult large ($5.25 each) x ____ (number required) $_____

    Adult extra large ($5.25 each) x ____ (number required) $_____

    Adult extra extra large ($7.00 each) x ____ (number required) $_____

6. Reunion Costs (postage, invitations, decorations, rent, etc.)

    $3.00 per person x _____number of people in party $_____

TOTAL COST $_____

Make all checks payable to **James McLaughlin**

Mail check and this form to **James McLaughlin, 12345 Howard Street, Anywhere, ND 00000**

RSVP please. REMEMBER, **THE DEADLINE FOR RESERVATIONS IS APRIL 1, 1994.**

Your name: _____

Address: _____

City: _____ **State:** _____ **Zip:** _____

Phone: _____ **Number of people attending:** _____

FOOD

Food is an important part of most family reunions -- breaking bread together. A potluck meal, in which everyone brings a dish to share, is the most common way to handle a meal for a gathering. You could also have the affair catered or go to a restaurant. Be sure to ask if there are any special dietary requirements (for health or religious reasons) that you should know about.

When the three-generation Ingram family holds their reunions in condos in Florida or Arkansas everyone is responsible for providing their own breakfast in their own condo. "Lunch is usually sandwiches, or snacks, or fast food, usually in the largest condo," says the patriarch of the family, Alvin Ingram. "Dinner is served twice by each family, again in the largest condo, and we take them all out to a nice restaurant at least once for a good meal."

If you are planning a potluck meal, be sure someone brings the accessories: salt, pepper, ice, condiments, butter, ketchup, mustard. Let everyone know whether they should bring their own plates, silverware, cups, napkins, and drinks, or whether the reunion committee will be supplying them. Make a list ahead of time of items you will need to rent or borrow: folding chairs, tables, canopy, ice chests, large coffee pot, etc. Often churches will loan folding tables and chairs to their members for backyard family gatherings. Don't hesitate to ask for help in the kitchen on the day of the event; many people enjoy themselves most when they are making a contribution.

Some families use a system to insure that a variety of food types are brought; for instance, everyone whose first name starts with A-F is asked to bring hot dishes, G-M salads, N-R desserts, S-V beverages, and W-Z condiments. In other families people might resent being told what to bring. It's up to you to determine what works for your family.

"The hosting family for our reunions provides the meat," says Mary Garbutt of Idaho. "The first generation -- the original brothers and sisters -- bring casseroles or baked beans. The children -- all cousins -- bring salads, and their children bring desserts."

Carolyn Surine reports that each family brings their own table service, meat to cook, and a dish to pass. "The local organizers brought gas grills, provided coffee pots and hot chocolate, and assisted those who needed to barbecue," she says. "One organizer brought a toddler wading pool where we put bags of ice to keep things cold."

John Rickey of Oklahoma says, "We have a hamburger fry or sandwiches for one meal, done by the host group, and those eating donate to the kitty. The other meal is a buffet at the resort."

Saturday night wiener roasts are popular at weekend reunions. After eating hot dogs with all the fixings, marshmallows are toasted on the campfire for dessert as family members gather around to sing favorite old songs and share stories about ancestors.

The Kelly Reunion holds a cooking contest as a source of food and fun at their reunions: a Meat Cook-off Contest for the grandsons, and a Dessert Cook-off for the granddaughters. Outside judges are used and the winners are presented with specially designed aprons. The Hammrick Clan holds an annual Chili Cook-off contest at their reunion, awarding a trophy to the winner. The chili entries and hot dogs become the evening meal.

At one reunion to encourage mingling during the meal, people are handed colored paper plates. They then sit at the table with the tablecloth that matches their plate. The Coburn Reunion uses charts to assign meal preparation tasks so that immediate families don't work together; this gives everyone a good opportunity to get acquainted with their other relatives, which is after all what reunions are all about.

Checklist for Organizing Your Family Reunion

Use the following checklist to keep track of what stage your plans need to be in for the reunion. Check off only the items that apply to the type of reunion you are planning.

Need to do   **Done**

ONE YEAR OR MORE BEFORE REUNION:

❑   ❑   Hold a preliminary meeting of core organizers to discuss general plans. Find out who is willing to help with the work.

❑   ❑   If available, read the notes from the person who organized the last reunion.

❑   ❑   Start a mailing list.

❑   ❑   Set date, location, and length of reunion.

❑   ❑   Choose and reserve facilities (lodging, meeting, food).

❑   ❑   Make a budget and determine costs (approximating on the high side when necessary).

❑   ❑   Send out first notification mailer; ask people to spread the word and help locate missing people. Give an approximate cost.

❑   ❑   Begin working on any large projects, such as a family cookbook.

❑   ❑   Choose the theme.

SIX TO TWELVE MONTHS BEFORE REUNION:

❑   ❑   Form committees: entertainment, registration, food, etc.

❑   ❑   Make a "Things-To-Do" checklist.

❑   ❑   Make a schedule of events and activities.

❑   ❑   Confirm reservations.

❑   ❑   Update mailing lists as people are located.

❑   ❑   Check into possible imprinted mementos to be given out or sold at the reunion.

❑   ❑   Make arrangements for band, tours, guest speakers, photographer, group rates to roller-skating facility, etc.

❑   ❑   Send the second mailer. Include registration form, exact costs, order form for souvenirs, information about any contests which will be held or special displays for which they should bring something, map, etc.

❑   ❑   Make a list of all items you will need to borrow or rent (folding chairs, large coffee pot, microphone, photocopier, etc.) and where to get them.

TWO TO SIX MONTHS BEFORE THE REUNION:

❑ ❑ Finalize any souvenirs or mementos.

❑ ❑ Decide on decorations, signs, banners.

❑ ❑ Check progress and problems of all committees.

❑ ❑ Assign reunion day tasks to people (registration table, transporting borrowed equipment, etc.).

❑ ❑ Reserve any rental equipment.

❑ ❑ Meet with hotel staff, caterer, band, etc. for final decisions.

❑ ❑ Send final mailer.

❑ ❑ Collect items for souvenir packet for each attendee.

ONE TO TWO MONTHS BEFORE THE REUNION:

❑ ❑ Review and revise schedule of events.

❑ ❑ Create a final checklist.

TWO WEEKS BEFORE THE REUNION:

❑ ❑ Buy decorations.

❑ ❑ Make name tags.

❑ ❑ Buy awards and gifts.

❑ ❑ Assign clean-up duties.

❑ ❑ Stock your first aid kit.

❑ ❑ Check to see that you have supplies for all planned activities.

❑ ❑ Review final checklist.

ONE TO TWO DAYS BEFORE THE REUNION:

❑ ❑ Coordinator and committee members meet to go over final details.

❑ ❑ Recheck arrangements for food, lodging, meeting place, entertainment.

❑ ❑ Stuff souvenir packets.

TWO TO TWENTY-FOUR HOURS BEFORE THE REUNION:

❑ ❑ Inspect meeting room for agreed-upon size, tables, chairs, layout, electronic and other accessory equipment.

❑ ❑ Provide hotel or caterer with final number of meals required.

❑ ❑ Check all borrowed or rented equipment to see that it is present and in working order.

❑ ❑   Check to see if reunion day workers have any questions about their duties.

❑ ❑   Hang banners and decorate; Set up displays, registration table, etc.

❑ ❑   Place any needed directional signs in hotel lobby or along road.

DURING THE REUNION:

☑ ❑   Enjoy! Be flexible!

AFTERWARDS:

❑ ❑   Clean up.

❑ ❑   Return rented and borrowed items.

❑ ❑   Reflect and evaluate. What went right and what didn't? Make notes for whoever organizes the next reunion.

❑ ❑   Write thank-you notes to volunteers and others.

❑ ❑   Pay bills.

During the Reunion

Advance planning will help your reunion run smoothly; imagination will make it sparkle! Incorporate the unique charm and character of your family into the reunion plans. Celebrate your heritage and accomplishments. No other family in the world is quite like yours -- the saints and the scamps included.

Decide what the purpose (or purposes) of this particular reunion is before planning activities for it. Is it an opportunity for members of the clan to visit and catch up on what is happening in each other's lives? Is it a chance for newly found branches of the family to be introduced to everyone else? Are you celebrating a particular event, anniversary, or milestone? Do you want to use the gathering to further genealogical research? Is there a project or task which you would like the family to work on as a group? Keep that purpose in mind while browsing through the rest of this book. Hundreds of ideas are included; choose those which will help you accomplish your goal.

One word of caution: Don't organize every available moment of the reunion. Allow plenty of time for socializing.

REGISTRATION

Consider setting up a check-in table at your reunion. It provides a convenient place to have everyone sign the guest book, pay any reunion fees that are being charged, pass out reunion packets and name tags, ask for any address corrections for your mailing list, and distribute any souvenirs (such as imprinted t-shirts) which the attendees ordered in advance. By handling this task as soon as the person arrives, it will be easier to keep track of who has received the souvenirs and who hasn't.

The reunion packet for each person or family could include: a directory of all descendants with the names of the spouses, children, addresses, and telephone numbers; reunion program; map with directions to all events; souvenir notepad printed with reunion letterhead; pencil; compressed pedigree chart for their family branch; pertinent facts about nearby tourist attractions; police and hospital numbers; directions to local parks and shopping centers; hotel regulations; and list of nearby restaurants.

"A Welcome Booklet was given to everyone upon arrival (at the Sarine-Sirrine-Surine Family Association reunion)," says Carolyn Surine of New York. "It was intended to provide a little fun information and to be a keepsake of the reunion, as well as serve as an orientation/scheduling tool." The booklet contained a reunion schedule, welcome message, space for taking notes, etc.

Many families make some sort of 'We Have Arrived' display at the registration table so that each person can easily see who has already arrived. This could be a large tree -- without foliage -- drawn or painted on foam core board; arriving relatives write their names on leaf cut-outs and attach them to the branches of the tree with stickpins. Or, instead of leaves, the names are written on red posterboard apples or hearts and the tree has plenty of green foliage painted on it for a pretty background.

Sometimes a puzzle is used. Each piece of the puzzle has the name of a person or family written on it. Trace all of the pieces in the assembled position on a piece of cardboard. Instruct each person to place his or her puzzle piece in position on the outline upon arrival. Another creative alternative is to design a hanging mobile which can be added to, piece by piece. Each tier of the mobile indicates a generation.

If signs are needed to direct people to the registration table, hospitality room, or wherever, you can make portable, free-standing signs with bleach or milk jugs, sand, long lathes or sticks, and posterboard. Fill the jugs with sand and insert the sticks. Staple the appropriate sign to the wood lathe.

Figure 4. One 8 1/2" x 14" sheet of paper can be folded into quarters to form a four-page program booklet, a nice memento of the day.

PROGRAM

10:00 Registration, Socializing

12:00 Blessing & Lunch

1:00 Program
1. Welcome
2. Roll call of elders
3. Announcements
4. Skit by H. cousins
5. Solo by Julie H.
6. Reading by Fred H.

2:00 Family Portraits

2:30 Family Olympics (competition between the four branches of the family, all ages participate in a variety of competition!)

4:00 Cake cutting

DID YOU KNOW...

...that our ancestor Frank Hindenburg came from Germany with $50, two changes of clothing, his carpentry tools, and a great desire to be an American.

...Frank and Angeline were both the 4th child of a 4th child.

...Angeline played the organ for their church for 35 years.

...the elaborate cross at the front of the church was lovingly carved by Frank in 1927.

...Frank and Angeline had 4 children who had 12 children who had 38 children who so far have had 6 children!

...that the first official reunion for the Hindenburg Family was held in 1942.

A note from Grandma Audrey –

I remember my father telling me about the first Hindenburg reunion. Grandpa Frank had everyone hold hands and form a circle. The circle was silent as Grandpa looked around.

"32 Americans," he said. "32 Hindenburgs."

He turned to Grandma Angeline. "The Book says to be fruitful and multiply, Momma," he said smiling. "I guess we did!"

Grandpa gave the blessing and then he and Grandma sat on the glider on the porch, holding hands and watching their descendants help themselves to Grandma's wonderful German dishes.

The 1993 Hindenburg Family Reunion

Celebrating
100 Years
in
America

ELBURN FOREST PRESERVE · AUG. 7

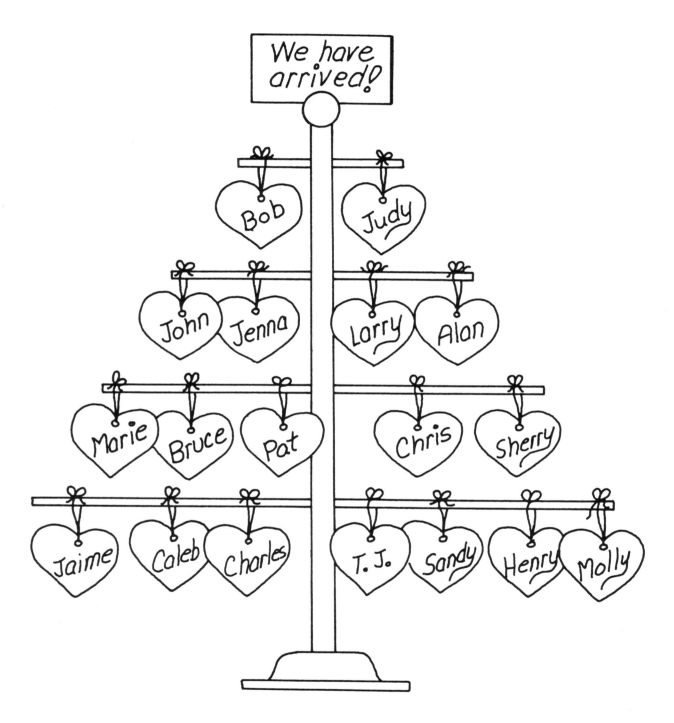

Figure 5. Ask everyone to hang a personalized wood heart on a wood dowel tree as they arrive. The tree can be made as large as necessary. The trunk of this four-tier tree is a 1 1/4" diameter dowel. The wood ball on top is slotted to hold the card. A carved scrap of 2x4 and an oval wood plaque form the base. 5/8" diameter dowels are inserted into four snug fitting holes drilled through the trunk, making them removeable for easier storage between reunions.

Figure 6. Here is one method of numbering family members, useful for quickly showing family relationships on name tags. The first generation has one number (1). The second generation has two numbers (1-1, 1-2, 1-3), and so on. Spouses are indicated with an 's' after the number.

Descendants of Ernest & Rebecca Jones

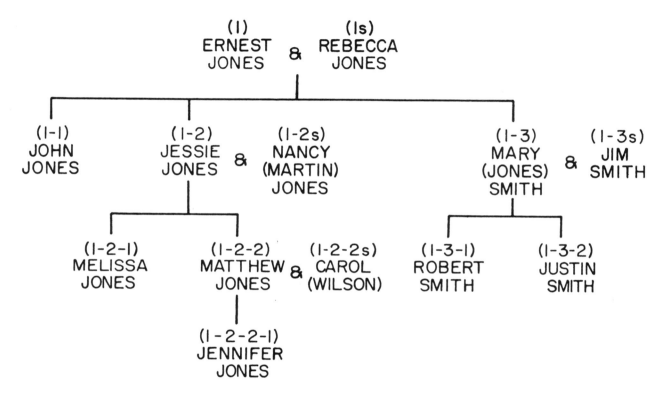

NAME TAGS

Name tags are essential at large reunions, and helpful even at medium to small reunions. They can prevent embarrassing moments such as when someone greets us enthusiastically but we can't remember their name. Even if the majority of the people are already acquainted with each other, the new spouse or the person from another branch of the family who decided to attend your reunion will really appreciate your thoughtfulness in providing name tags to help them learn everyone's name. Name tags on children are especially helpful; their looks change so much from one year to the next that it is hard to keep track of who belongs to whom. One disadvantage of name tags on children, however, is that it allows anyone to call them by their name -- even strangers with bad intentions -- so please use caution.

There are a variety of types of name tags: metal, plastic, stick-on, and those which hang from a string around the neck. Generally they are color coded to aid in identification, such as the coding method used at the Dahler Family Reunion:

"Our immigrant family had eight branches," says Carol Wilson of Wisconsin. "We asked one person to head each branch and we gave each a different colored ribbon to wear."

Figures 7-12. Six styles of name tags. The Jennifer Jones in Figure 6 is used for the example.

Figure 7

·1·2·2·1·
JENNIFER JONES

Cleveland, OH

Figure 8

JENNIFER JONES

daughter of
Matthew & Carol Jones

Figure 9

JENNIFER JONES

Matthew Jones
Jessie Jones
Ernest Jones

Figure 10

Ernest Jones
Jessie Jones
Matthew Jones

JENNIFER JONES

Jones Reunion 1993

Figure 11

Figure 12

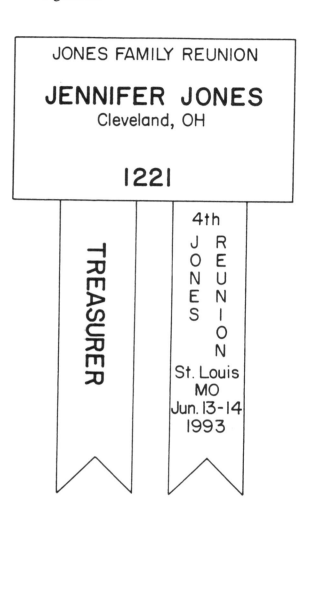

Sometimes family logos are used on the name tag. The Rickey Reunion used a 2 1/2" circular, yellow button with the family's covered wagon logo in the center. Around the edge of the button was imprinted "Rickey Revel II, Jun 1991, Portsmouth, OH". A ribbon suspended from the button identified each person by name and home state.

Jo Ann Casebier of Kansas reports that her family made name tags for the doors of each cabin or room at the Coburn Reunion, telling who the occupants were. "Be sure to list your parent's name under your own name to help everyone understand how they fit into the family," she advises.

At the Santellanes-Sandoval Reunion the color coding extended to the clothing worn by family members. "My grandparents had seven children," says Rosie Santellanes Grice of Arizona. "Each branch of the tree was assigned a different color -- pink, blue, green, turquoise, purple, red, and yellow. Guests were instructed to wear black or white. Each family was responsible for deciding what kind of shirt, how they should be bought, what logo they want on it, etc. The color coding system readily allowed everyone to identify who belonged to what branch."

Color coding of clothing can also be useful during family games and when taking group pictures.

WELCOMING EVERYONE AND GETTING ACQUAINTED

Some families begin welcoming people to the reunion before the person even arrives. At one reunion held in a rural area a series of signs was placed along the route that most people would take to get to the farm. Large print messages such as "ONLY TWO MORE MILES TO GO TO THE BEST REUNION YOU'LL EVER ATTEND" and "ONLY ONE MORE MILE TO THE FRIENDLIEST (surname)'S ON EARTH!" were painted on the plywood signs.

Hang banners and balloons at the reunion site. See page 48 for instructions on how to make one reunion banner that is sure generate its share of smiles. Signs such as "HUGS ARE THE SPECIALTY OF THE JOHNSON FAMILY. WE ENCOURAGE RETURNS! ONE SIZE FITS ALL" also enhance the family spirit.

It is helpful to have a designated greeter at the reunion to ensure that everyone is enthusiastically welcomed. Don't have people standing on the sidelines, just watching. Help them interact and get acquainted.

"Our aim is to keep the reunion perpetuated," says Milton Autry of the Autry Family Association, "so we've been trying to see that each age group gets introduced, then they seem to quickly find things they have in common, etc. When a person comes for the first time we try to get him/her under the wing of someone in the same age group who will try to keep bringing the newcomer into different conversations. I have noticed a positive difference the last two or three years. The first few reunions the only people greeting them as they arrived were the appointed ones. Now it seems that everyone keeps an eye on the entrance door and can hardly wait until they get registered before crowding around them."

For one reason or another relatives are often shy with each other after being out of touch for a long time. Mixer games such as Hello Bingo (page 151) can help them get comfortable with each other again and also get newcomers involved. Conversation pieces such as a scale model of a family house (page 78) give people something to talk about during those first few minutes.

One family which gave out randomly colored name tags (instead of color-coding them to the branches of the family) got people talking during the reunion reception by asking everyone with a certain color name tag to get in a group and get acquainted. They were told that after five minutes one person in the group would be asked to introduce another person from the group and tell who they are, where they are from, and how they are related.

Trying to prevent families from staying in their own little groups instead of meeting other relatives, many of whom may be strangers, is a real challenge but challenges are the spice of life! Remind everyone of the five best things to bring to a reunion: a smile, a hug, the phrase "I'm so glad to see you!", an open mind, and willingness to help out in any way needed.

THEME

You might want to pick a unifying theme for the reunion and carry through with colors, entertainment, activities, and food. Some possible themes are: "Getting to know all about you", family keepsakes and collectibles, occupations -- past and present, serving our country, special traditions

Figure 13. Beautiful old marriage certificates could be displayed at a reunion with a wedding theme. Encourage everyone to bring wedding photos and tell stories of old-time shivarees.

and customs, passing down old-time crafts and childhood games, celebrating our ethnic heritage, how we made it through the depression and other disasters, and family myths and legends.

Plan activities around the theme. You could have a human scarecrow contest and a hayride for a Down-on-the-farm theme. The children could put on a nativity pageant for a Christmas-in-July theme; take instant snapshots of them to use in making Christmas tree ornaments. (See page 109 for more Christmas theme ideas.) The year Brenda Gotensky's family had a Christmas-in-July theme they rented a union hall and celebrated it just like Christmas with a tree, gifts, Santa, and all. Some other themes this family has used are the "Gay Nineties," wedding anniversary celebration, country and western, and a Hawaiian West Virginia Holiday.

The theme for one Frisbie/Frisbee Annual Reunion was "Frisbies in the Civil War Era". The organizers asked family members to "...delve into your family history and remember or discover what your family ancestors were doing during the times of the Civil War. Bring your stories and mementos to share".

Ruth Brown of Indiana says, "One year everyone came dressed 'old fashioned' and had our pictures taken." You might want to hold an old-time party which includes such things as pulling taffy and making homemade ice cream in a handcrank freezer. Let all the children have a turn at the crank. Don't forget the other oldies but goodies: pitching horseshoes and a watermelon seed spitting contest!

A decorated cake which indicates the theme of the reunion is a nice touch. Give the honor of cutting the first piece to the host or the oldest relative present, and have your cameras ready.

DISPLAYS

Special displays at a family reunion can be interesting, informative, and excellent conversation-starters. Ask people to bring old photographs or memorabilia. Provide a 'sharing table' where family members can display family memorabilia (family Bibles, reunion scrapbook, etc.) and the products of their own talents (a wood carving, handmade quilt, framed poem, etc.).

Photo 1: Courtesy of Bert Frye.
Displayed at the Frey Family Reunion are dolls dressed in mid-1700s style of clothing
to represent two ancestors, and a document about the immigration of another.

"We had a memory 'photo wall' in the garage, consisting of dozens of old photos displayed in clear plastic pocket photo holders," says Beverly Bauda of New York. "This was a true walk down memory lane for everyone."

You could use large sheets of foam core board and mount photos with photo corners (so that they can be removed easily afterwards). Write captions underneath or beside them. A room divider could also be used. Some families wrap the board with clear plastic (such as used in window winterizing kits) to protect the photos from theft and fingerprints.

Diane Brown of Alabama says, "We couldn't find a copier to rent for two days and some people wouldn't bring their precious pictures to share, but before the reunion they went to a copy place and made color copies. (Some regular copiers have a photo button). I also wrote in the information letter that if someone didn't have access to a copier I would be glad to make copies and return the information at the reunion. Several older relatives were unable to come, but sent me boxes of precious LABELED pictures. I thought I was in heaven!!! We placed these copies on a table, but labeled each section as to which family of our ancestors these belonged."

Large family tree displays are usually a big hit at reunions. At the Lillibridge Family Reunion a 24-foot-long pedigree chart for the first five generations of the family was displayed on the wall. On a table below the chart were placed the family genealogist's notebooks (10 linear feet) which were keyed to numbers on the wall chart. In the notebooks were pictures, obituaries, census records, etc. on individuals within the family.

Encourage children to make displays for the reunion also. They could use a U.S. or world map to show how the family has moved around, or make a timeline to show past family events. They could also make a wall hanging 'quilt' which uses wallpaper instead of fabric for the blocks and ink instead of embroidery.

PROGRAM

Family reunion programs can be very planned, very impromptu, or anything in between. It's a good idea to have a master of ceremonies to help it run smoothly and tie everything together. Be mindful of how long little ones can sit still if children will be attending the program; perhaps you will want to plan some intense physical activities for them just before the program so that they will be ready to sit and rest awhile.

Programs often start with a prayer and/or a roll call. Henrietta Evans of Ohio reports, "We call the sixteen children of ancestor William (first in this country) tribes and have a roll call."

Sometimes the Lord's Prayer and the Pledge of Allegiance are recited to begin a reunion program. Often the reunion president stands and asks for the names of any additions to the family during the preceding year, thereby recognizing the new babies and new spouses. The names of those who have died during the year are then asked for and acknowledged. This is helpful for updating the family history book; those with announcements to contribute are asked to submit the specifics to the family historian.

Diane Brown of Alabama reports about the planned program at her family reunions: "Each family (children's families of my great-great-grandmother) has a spokesperson who stands at the microphone and gives a little history of their ancestor, announces any births, deaths, or marriages since the last reunion, and any memories they want to share. No more than five or six minutes each."

Mary Garbutt of Idaho adds: "In the last few years we've made each of the 'Old Folks' stand up in order and tell something along the line of 'What my brothers and sisters did to me when I was a kid' or 'The worst trouble I ever got into' or 'Favorite memory of my father'."

Ruth Brown of Indiana describes a little about the Boehm family reunion: "One year after the dinner we had a show-and-tell time. Each person brought something old and told about it and why it meant so much to them. That was really super."

Talent shows and skits are popular at reunions. John Lillibridge comments on one of the Lillibridge family reunions: "The highlight of the day was a guest speaker, not previously identified to anyone, who was dressed in the costume of the immigrant ancestor. He gave a ten minute talk, set in the language of 1724, about his family and his life in America. Many of his descendants wanted their picture taken with him."

One member of the Allison family reunion, Lois Allison Shelton, also donned an appropriate costume to do an impersonation of an ancestor -- her great-grandmother, Mary Ragsdale Allison. This would be a wonderful highlight for any family reunion program!

Sometimes there are guest speakers. "One year we were fortunate to have a lady from Scotland speak and she was great," says Mary Cathey Summers of North Carolina.

Video presentations are very popular, especially at gatherings with a genealogical purpose such as the National Fry(e) Reunion:

"During our evening program my son presented a 40-minute video production regarding our family's participation on several American frontiers and our contribution in a developing nation," says Bert Frye of Ohio.

The slide presentation at the Dahler Family Reunion showed the ship their immigrant family arrived on and some old letters from the family who stayed behind. At medium to small reunions you might ask people to bring slides on a specific subject -- first birthday of all grandchildren, graduation, wedding pictures, etc. If someone in the family is interested in old homes or towns of ancestors they could visit these structures and places and take pictures. Photos of old-timers who remember the family could also be included and their story told while the slides are being shown.

Many reunion programs include a memorial service: "We have an easel poster board to put all of the family members' names that are deceased on," says Martha Grubbs of Kentucky. "We have a memorial service from 11 A.M. to 12 noon." This group also performs a family musical. All family members who wish to participate practice for the musical for about one and a half hours on Saturday night, and perform at whichever church they have chosen at 3 P.M. on Sunday. "In the January meeting we usually vote on what church to have the musical at," says Martha. "It is usually a church from one of the family members here in Paducah."

The Robinett Reunion also includes a memorial service. It is held at the church where a Robinett marriage took place in 1653, and is planned by the church minister around songs and sermons of that time.

The DeHaven reunion included a variety of events, as described by Carolyn Cokerham of Texas: "We were brought together by media coverage concerning a lawsuit against the government for repayment of a 214-year-old loan made to George Washington by a member of our family. We found 1400 family members. Friday night was fiesta, music and food. Saturday was Revolutionary War Fife and Drum Corps, speeches, recognition of those over eighty, Sweet Adelines Barbershop group, raffle, sale of family t-shirts, glassware, hats, etc., panoramic photo of all in attendance, BBQ lunch, recognition of the thirty-eight states present, visitation time, children's t-shirt painting, piñatas, and color books. There was a play with Betsy Ross, George Washington, and Uncle Jacob to tell the family history. We had a genealogy set up separate from the reunion festivities. There was a hour period of time set up for exchange of info, etc."

Many other reunions schedule a certain amount of time for exchanging genealogical information; for others this is the sole purpose of the gathering.

"Since 1987 we have had a gathering on Saturday before the reunion for those who are interested in their genealogy," says Mary Cathey Summers of North Carolina. "This is usually scheduled at the Holiday Inn where most of the family members are staying."

Diane Brown of Alabama found her family reunion to be the solution to her problem of trying to collect family information:

"I had been working on our family tree for years, but couldn't get everyone to supply the needed information," she says. "All it took was one reunion where out beside their ancestor's name was 'Information Not Received'. I received most of the needed information within a month or two!"

If genealogical research is part or all of your reunion activities you may want to rent a photocopier for the convenience of everyone present. Don't depend on the hotel office for this service. Arrange for the pick-up and delivery of the rented machine. Make sure you have plenty of paper, and that someone is designated to learn how to clear jams, etc. You also might want to check to see if the copier you will be renting has a special button for copying photos.

Having a variety of activities helps to ensure that everyone will find something to enjoy. Sometimes the location itself is a major part of the program, as was the case of the Stanton Reunion. It was held at a farm which was founded in 1654 by Thomas Stanton and now owned by John (Whit) Davis, who met a Stanton daughter, married, and then bought the farm. Thomas Stanton had a trading post and was an official Indian interpreter for the Crown. The reunion was billed as the first Stanton Reunion in 337 years. The three-day event was held in a large field across from the 320-year-old house built by Thomas Stanton. The 262 family members and friends who attended enjoyed a steer pit-barbecue, venison stew, chowder, chicken, and square dancing. Electricity and portable outhouses were available for those who wished to camp on the farm.

Photo 2: Courtesy of Nyla Stanton. Attendees at the Stanton Reunion gather for a peace ceremony with a member of the same Indian tribe that once traded with their ancestor.

Photo 3: Courtesy of Bernard Stanton. Grey Wolf (Richard Harris) burns a mixture of sage, sweetgrass, and cedar at the ceremony to signify purity, promote relaxation, and aid in meditation.

Photo 4: Courtesy of Bernard Stanton. Smoking the peace pipe during the ceremony.

Photo 5: Courtesy of Nyla Stanton. Roasting beef over an open pit at the Stanton Reunion.

Photo 6: Courtesy of Bernard Stanton. Stanton Reunion activities included hay rides with Belgian horses and a tour of the family farm and cemetery.

Usually a business meeting needs to be conducted at some time during the reunion in order to discuss next year's reunion, elect officers, decide on family projects, discuss the possibility of incorporating the association, etc. The Harris Reunion holds their business meeting after dinner:

"During the business meeting the younger children are taken across the street to the park to swim or use the playground equipment depending on age and interest level," says Jo Ann Casebier of Kansas. "There is also a nice pond in the park where the younger children like to feed the ducks. The teenagers are responsible for the younger children during the business meeting so that their parents can participate in the meeting. Everyone stays for the opening of the meeting and group pictures and then they are dismissed."

At another reunion a clown is hired to manage the children's games while the business meeting is going on.

Whenever people congregate there is always the problem of noise, especially during programs. It is very frustrating to watch an obviously interesting and entertaining program but not be able to hear it. Consider renting a speaker system if one is not already available at your reunion location.

"At our first reunion the PA system wasn't adequate to be heard over the buzz of the crowd," says Don Thomson of Maryland. "Apparently people were too busy getting acquainted to be still during the use of the PA system. An amplified speech system is definitely a must and should be tested ahead of time."

TOURS TO LOCAL PLACES OF INTEREST

Are there historical houses of interest to the family in the area? Consider planning a tour of them and also such places as the store that Grandpa once owned and the old school. Allow enough time for those who want to take pictures.

"We have an open house the preceding Saturday night at the original home of Samuel and Sarah Lamb, now inhabited by a descendant," says George Carlisle of the Lamb family reunion. "They usually have a cake decorated with 'Lamb Family' and a picture of a lamb. There is a photograph of Samuel Lamb in the foyer; the northwest parlor on the first floor still has the original plaster and wainscoting woodwork. There is a widow's walk on the roof, which the family goes up on to look at the flat farmland and the trees to the north on the bluffs of the Mississippi River."

Ruth Brown of Indiana reports, "One year we made up a map of the area, showing where all of our ancestors had lived, had businesses, gone to school, and any other important events in their lives. We then drove to each place, told about the importance of it, and allowed pictures to be taken if they wished. We even visited the cemeteries for the out-of-state relatives to see and know all about them."

The organizers of the Dahler Reunion included a list of family members buried there with printed directions on how to get to the cemetery.

CONTESTS, AWARDS, DOOR PRIZES

Holding a contest is a great way to increase active participation by family members in the reunion. Check Chapter VI Recreation Ideas for suggestions such as a Baby Picture contest and the Family Olympics. Hold a crazy hat contest or a recycled costume contest (see page 139).

The Kelly Reunion, held the third or fourth weekend in October, includes a Halloween Costume Contest on Saturday evening:

"There are outside judges," says Mary Katherine Townsend of Texas, "and small trophies and/or ribbons are awarded in a number of categories -- Prettiest, Most Original, etc. We keep our costumes secret. It's a lot of fun. Even older folks (70-80 years old) participate. All children receive a ribbon. Our judges are creative at finding labels for them all, such as Prettiest Little Unicorn."

The Kelly family also holds a Cook-off Contest for grandsons and granddaughters on Sunday. "This year we are adding a Jr. Cook-off Contest for great grandchildren," says Mary. "Outside judges are used and we set a specific time for judging."

Reunion organizers often plan miscellaneous awards to present during the program: to the person traveling the farthest, the newest married, the longest married, the youngest, the oldest male and female in attendance, the person who has attended the most reunions, the person with the most children and grandchildren present, the first one to sign the reunion book, etc.

"Sometimes prizes are given for the one with the biggest head, the one with the biggest shoe, the one with the biggest waistline, the man with the smallest waistline, etc.," says Roberta Mingyar of West Virginia. "Measuring is done by several persons with tapes and calling out the measurements for everyone to hear!"

Photo 7: Courtesy of Mary Katherine Townsend. Special aprons are awarded to the winners of the Kelly Reunion cooking contest.

A 'True Grit Award' was given at the Lemaster/Patterson Reunion to a person who had weathered cancer and was doing fine; the award appropriately had a piece of sandpaper on it. At the Lamb Family Reunion a lamb cake mold is given to the couple most recently married, and a stuffed toy lamb to the youngest person.

"There is a Lamb prize for the reddest hair, a family trait," says George Carlisle of Illinois. "I found a homemade lamb 'piggy' bank at a garage sale and painted the white fleece primer-coat red, which just about matches Justin Kaiser's hair."

Photo 8: Courtesy of George Carlisle.
The Lamb family award for the reddest hair--held by the winner.

Many of the prizes in one family are notecards with the family emblem embossed on them -- an encouragement for keeping in touch.

Door prizes are popular, with the names of the winners drawn from a container which includes the name of each person present. Sometimes numbers are taped to the bottom of certain chairs in the banquet room and whoever is sitting in that chair when the numbers are drawn wins a prize -- often the centerpiece on that table.

Everyone looks forward to the door prizes at the reunion of the Lilly Clan of Oregon: "In our letter of invitation families are asked to bring a donation," says William Hundley of Oregon. "Tickets are handed out on arrival. We gave away all sorts, paintings, kitchen utensils, car washing kits, wine, pies, cash, etc."

The *Reunions* magazine (P.O. Box 11727, Milwaukee, WI 53211-0727) is currently offering door prizes for reunions, meetings, conferences, and conventions. The prize includes a copy of the magazine and a certificate for a one-year subscription. If you would like to request a door prize for your reunion send in your name and address, tell where and when the prize will be presented, and how many are expected to attend.

RECORDING THE EVENT

Cameras usually abound at reunions; no reunion is complete without the taking of photographs -- posed groups and impromptu snapshots. When planning the layout of your meeting area, consider setting up an appropriate area for taking group photographs. Diane Brown of Alabama has a suggestion this activity:

"When we make family group pictures I make large posterboard signs for each family to have in their picture. It says 'Descendants of _____.' Then when I get the pictures I send one to the contact person in that family and they identify them. At one time we tried to write down by rows who was in the picture, but it took too much time."

Another way to identify people in a group is to videotape them while still in position and have each person state their name.

Figure 14. Identify people in a group photo by placing tracing paper over the photo and tracing a rough outline of the head and shoulders of each person. Number these outlines and list the names below.

1. William Rescott	8. Kim Anderson
2. Jennifer Rescott	9. Matthew Rescott
3. Barry Anderson	10. Jaime Anderson
4. John Rescott	11. Rebecca Rescott
5. Karen Anderson	12. George Rescott
6. Laura Rescott	13. Nancy Rescott
7. Dakota Rescott	14. Nathaniel Rescott

Many families have a formal portrait taken of the group by a professional photographer every so many years; orders are taken for copies. If you plan to do this, be sure your photographer has had experience photographing large groups of people. If proper care isn't taken many people will end up partially hidden in the photograph.

Reunions where color-coded clothing is worn to distinguish different family branches have particularly interesting group photos: "Each family group wore different color t-shirts for the pictures," says Lois Schafer of Nebraska. "We had black, blue, light blue, red, maroon, green, and navy."

Don't forget notebooks, tape recorders, and camcorders when making a record of the reunion. An oral family history taping session can be fun to do and will become a cherished keepsake for all who get copies of it. Ask each person to tell something that they remember about the family's past. A list of suggestions can be helpful to get it started: Describe your childhood home. How did you meet your husband/wife? Describe an incident that happened while you were visiting relatives.

Two good books to consult for ideas on this type of activity are *Keeping Family Stories Alive: A Creative Guide to Recording Your Family Life and Lore* by Vera Rosenbluth (Point Roberts, Washington: Hartley & Marks, 1990) and *Video Family Portraits: the User Friendly Guide to Video Taping Your Family History, Stories, and Memories* by Rob Huberman and Laura Janis (Bowie, Maryland: Heritage Books, Inc., 1987).

Photo 9: Courtesy of Bert Frye.

A large family reunion banner provides a great background for a group photo.

Photo 10: Don't forget to take some close-up photos.

OTHER ACTIVITIES

Watching home slides and movies are always popular at reunions, as long as it isn't done too often. One good way to make a VCR tape of 8-track home movies is to set up a camcorder to record what is being shown on the projector screen during the family viewing. A major advantage of doing this -- as opposed to having the movies commercially copied -- is that the microphone will also be recording the comments of the audience while they are watching it: identifying old people who are now dead, laughing at childhood antics, explaining why Aunt Matilda has Cousin Jane's young bridegroom by the scruff of the neck. What a wonderful background to listen to years from now!

You may want to set up a system so that people can order copies for themselves of old photographs which have been brought to the reunion; or perhaps ask a camera store for information on how to do this on site and rent or borrow the needed equipment. Another alternative is to rent a photocopier which has a special button for copying photographs.

If there is a particular old photograph of great sentimental or historic value but which is damaged, the family might want to check into using the services of a business that specializes in restoring and reproducing old photos. Look in your telephone book for listings. Two possibilities are:

Just Black & White
    P.O. Box 4628
    Portland, Maine 04112
        (800) 827-5881
        (207) 761-5861

Digital Design
    5835 Avenida Encinas
    Suite #121
    Carlsbad, CA 92008
        (619) 931-2630
        FAX (619) 931-2632

An automatic slide show was set up at the Himes-Shaffer Family Reunion:

"Snapshots of the reunion have been taken throughout the day during the past five years by my daughter," says Roberta Mingyar of West Virginia. "They have been made into slides and presented throughout the day via a slide projector. The projector is set up so that the pictures appear automatically and anyone can go at their leisure to view them."

Sometimes reunion activities involve a tradition: "We have a family plaque which is passed from one family to the next on a rotating basis yearly," says Mary Katherine Townsend of Texas. "When it's time to eat we make a huge circle and number off. Announcements are made, winners announced (of their cooking contest), the plaque passed, and finally the blessing."

If you hold your reunion in the same place every year consider planting a seedling and then photograph the whole family group beside the tree each year. Watch both the tree and your family grow year by year in the photographs.

Wanda Copeland of Indiana describes a drawing held at their family gatherings: "At our family reunion some years ago one of my brothers, who whittles, had a drawing for a few of his whittled items. 'It' started from that and has progressed to a real highlight of out reunions. We realize there were a lot of talented people in our group and most everyone wanted to share in bringing something for a drawing. We have one who paints, someone draws, crafts of all descriptions, etc. Whoever brings something for the drawing puts it on a table that's set aside for it and at one end we have small pieces of paper for names and a slotted box to put them in for the drawing. We have a special time about mid afternoon when everyone is to be on hand for the drawing."

Perhaps your family would be interested in burying its own time capsule. The Erie Landmark Company (4449 Brookfield Corporate Drive, Chantilly, VA 22021-1681) specializes in historic preservation products, including a line of time capsules.

Photo 11: Courtesy of Mary Katherine Townsend.
The Kelly Plaque is passed from one brother to another.

Activities that mix the generations are particularly appropriate and desirable at reunions. William Holland of California reports that the teams for the paddleboat and potato sack races at their reunions must include an oldster and a youngster. "We also have special drawings where family heirlooms are passed down to the younger people."

For reunions lasting two or more days you might want to arrange a group outing to a roller-skating rink, bowling alley, golf course, or a local county fair. Hold a dinner dance one evening or a family worship service on Sunday. Prepare an ice cream sundae-making table for the enjoyment of the children, or let them take a swing at a piñata. Play cards and talk all night. Enjoy each other!

Photo 12: Two sisters having fun with a grass skirt!

REUNION WRAP-UP

When the reunion is over it's time to clean up, pay bills, and send out thank you letters. Evaluate what worked, what didn't, and what could be improved. For the benefit of whoever will be in charge of the next reunion, jot down notes about this year's gathering for future reference.

Charles Bland of New York publishes a Reunion Special each year after the reunion. The *1992 Bland Family Reunion Special* included a narrative about reunion events, a list of those who attended, a letter from the governor of Colorado recognizing the Bland family's contributions to the U.S. and wishing them a happy reunion, a Proclamation from a Colorado senator which welcomed the Bland family to Colorado, and eighteen pages of photos taken at the reunion. It totaled thirty pages and sold for $16.

Figure 15. Courtesy of Ellie Anthenat. One mother passed out these questionnaires after a reunion to solicit comments about it.

EVALUATION SHEET

So, what do ya think? Circle the best answer; this is not a quiz.

1) The overall idea:

    great   so-so   yuck

Comment:_____

_____

2.) Place:

    just right   O.K.   all wrong

Comment:_____

_____

3) Time of year: yeah   nay

    Time of day: yeah   nay

Comment:_____

_____

4) Should we repeat this?

    all right!   fine   no way

Comment:_____

_____

5) How soon?

    1 year   2 years   5 years   never

Comment:_____

_____

6) What should be done differently?_____

_____

7) Any suggestions for improvement, or new ideas?_____

_____

<u>REUNION SPECIAL 1992</u>

EIGHTH NATIONAL BLAND REUNION,
AUGUST 13-16, 1992, DENVER COLORADO

"The Rocky Mountain Special"

This Reunion Is Dedicated to
The Honorable Richard Parks "Silver Dick" Bland

By

Charles L. Bland

Figure 16. Courtesy of Charles Bland. Front cover of the <u>1992 Bland Reunion Special</u>.

Decorations, Mementos, Special Touches

Frills such as decorations and mementos aren't a necessary part of a family reunion, but they can be a fun part and needn't be expensive. Freida Price of Illinois put her imagination to work and came up with a great souvenir for her reunion:

"My family name is Pinkston. It was Pinkstone in old England," she says. "Last year my cousin and I visited my grandparents' farm home in Missouri (they are deceased and someone else lives there now but we got permission) and picked up half dollar size reddish or pink stones from the creek there. Each was washed and placed in a small ziplock bag with a label -- 'My Pet Pinkstone from the Pinkston Reunion 1991'."

Many families provide unifying souvenirs such as commemorative t-shirts or sweatshirts at reunions with the name of the family reunion and the year printed on them. These could be custom ordered from a specialty t-shirt shop or made at home. Beverly Bauda's sister designed and made unique photo shirts for their reunion; she had old sepia-tone and black-and-white photos copied on a color copy machine (about $2.00 per sheet) and transferred them onto a solid color sweatshirt with a fabric transfer medium sold in craft stores for about $3-4 per bottle. She then painted the edges with fabric paint to look like ribbons and antique photo holders, and used real antique buttons for trim.

Letter openers, bumper stickers, hats, buttons, stationery, pencils, pop coolers, tote bags, and a number of other items have also been used as mementos with the family surname printed on them. Embroidered patches are popular. If you will be holding contests or games during the reunion your local print shop can make a supply of fill-in-the-blank awards which include the name and year of the reunion, printed on stock paper with elegant borders.

Some families have made a tradition out of certain decorations. A special touch at the Lemaster/Patterson Reunion is their reunion tablecloth: "A family tree is in the center," says Phyllis Rhodes of New Mexico. "Everyone has signed their name on it and one of the aunts has embroidered each name. Any newcomer is asked to sign the tablecloth."

Here are some ideas for reunion decorations or interesting conversation starters that require some advance planning and work, but are well worth the effort:

Photo 13: Courtesy of Fern Hill. The Lemaster/Patterson Reunion tablecloth.

FAMILY TREE CHARTS

A family tree chart displayed on the wall or on a table is always popular at large reunions. Members of the family who have computers may already have software capable of generating a chart which will help newcomers to the reunion (or regular goers who are only just beginning to have an interest in genealogy) see how everyone fits on the tree. You could also draw one by hand on plain paper or buy a fill-in-the-blank chart. The following companies offer blank family tree charts:

1. Barnette's Family Tree Book Co.
   1001 West Loop North
   Houston, TX 77055
      (713) 684-4633

2. Genealogy Enterprises
   P.O. Box 6625
   Lake Worth, FL 33461

3. Genealogy Unlimited, Inc.
   P.O. Box 537
   Orem, UT 84059-0537
      (801) 226-8971
      (800) 666-4363

4. Hearthstone Bookshop
   5735-A Telegraph Rd.
   Alexandria, VA 22303
      (707) 960-0086

5. InfoPress Ink
   P.O. Box 40431
   Nashville, TN 37204-0431

6. Kusek Genealogical Services
   P.O. Box 32060
   Shawnee Msn., KS 66212-2060
      (913) 383-2458

7. Ye Olde Genealogie Shoppe
   9605 Vandergriff Road
   P.O. Box 39128
   Indianapolis, IN 46239
      (317) 862-3330

FAMILY REUNION BANNER

Photo 14: A banner can be colorful and decorative, as well as help people find the right spot for the family gathering. Hang this banner on the rain shelter at the park or outside the convention room at the hotel and the family members will have no doubt as to whether they are in the right area!

MATERIALS REQUIRED:
Baroque Satin fabric, 45" wide:

2 yards of white	Green twisted or braided cord, 42" long
1 1/3 yards of peacock blue	Two 1/2" diameter wood rods, each 34" long
1 yard of banana yellow	Four wood beads or washers
1/2 yard of hot pink	Black laundry marker or fabric pen
1/2 yard of holly green	Embroidery floss in desired hair colors

INSTRUCTIONS:

1) Enlarge pattern for "APPLIQUED PIECES ON FAMILY REUNION BANNER". Transfer enlarged pattern to the appropriate fabric colors (eagle is yellow, "CHEER..." banner is white, base is green with two small pink areas, the shield is blue with white and pink stripes). To transfer, tape the enlarged pattern on a lightboard or window pane. Place the fabric over it and trace the design lightly. Or, you can use dressmaker's tracing paper. Cut out the design at least 1/4" larger all the way around to allow a seam to fold under. Trace the "CHEER, CHEER..." lettering onto the white banner with a black laundry marker.

Figure 17

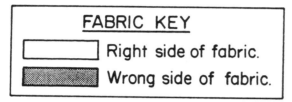

Figure 18

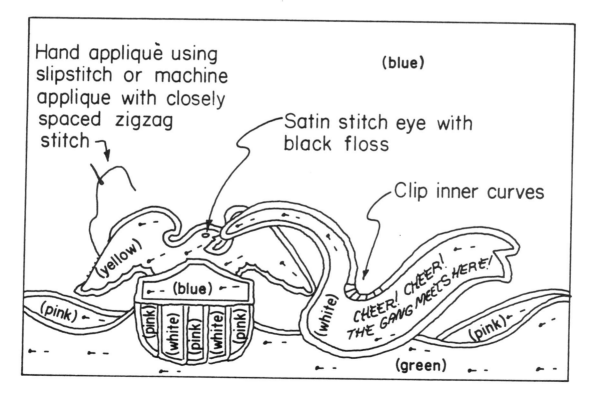

2) Cut two pieces of blue satin 33" x 22 1/2" (45" wide material cut in half). Pin the pieces to be appliqued on the right side of one of the pieces of blue satin (Fig. 18). Fold edges under -- to pattern line -- and sew on.

3) Enlarge the letters needed to spell the reunion name from "LETTERING FOR FAMILY REUNION BANNER". If you have a rather lengthy family name you can make the letters narrower than shown. Transfer enlarged letter patterns onto yellow satin and cut out at least 1/4" larger all around. Applique onto the area above the yellow eagle on the blue satin.

4) Take the two rectangles of blue satin, place right sides together and stitch side seams 1/2" from edge. Turn right side out. Press. Stitch top and bottom seams on right side, 1/4" from edge.

5) Cut four 3" x 33" strips of green satin, and eighteen 3" x 5" pieces of green satin. Fold the small pieces in half (Fig. 19) and sew 1/4" from edge. Turn right side out. Press, centering the seam in the middle of one side. Fold in half with the seam on the inside.

Figure 19

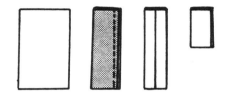

6) Space nine of these loops on the right side of one of the 33" strips, leaving 1/2" free at both ends. Place another 33" strip right side down on top and stitch 1/2" from edge (Fig. 20). Turn right side out and press. Repeat with the other two strips.

Figure 20

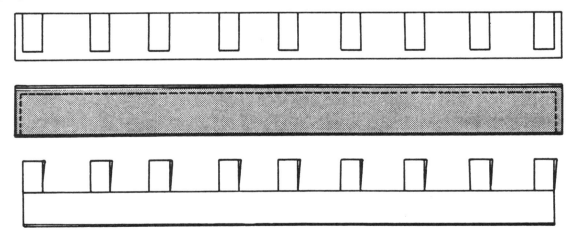

7) Place edge of looped strip at top of front side of banner (Fig. 21). Stitch 1/2" from edge. Finish by turning under 1/2" of the other edge and slipstitching to the back of the banner. Repeat for the bottom edge of the banner. Press.

Figure 21

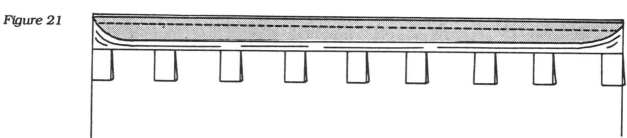

8) Insert wood rods at top and bottom. Finish the ends by attaching wood beads or washers with screws or strong glue. Tie the cord to the top rod and hang. (Note: You can prevent the banner from bunching up on the rod when waving in the breeze by fastening the two end loops to the rod with small tacks on the back side of the banner.)

9) Enlarge pattern for "PEOPLE ON FAMILY REUNION BANNER". Draw seven outlines for seven people. Add lines to indicate shorts, sleeves, etc., for a variety of clothing types. Transfer the enlarged patterns to the wrong side of the desired fabric colors, leaving at least 1/2" between pieces. DO NOT CUT OUT YET.

With right sides together sew fabric with traced patterns to another piece of fabric of the same color, stitching along pattern lines. Do not stitch the lines in between the fingers. Be sure to leave top of leg, bottom of hand or arm, and top and bottom of all clothing pieces open for turning (Fig. 22). Cut around pieces, staying 1/4" from seams, tops, and bottoms. Turn right side out and press.

Figure 22

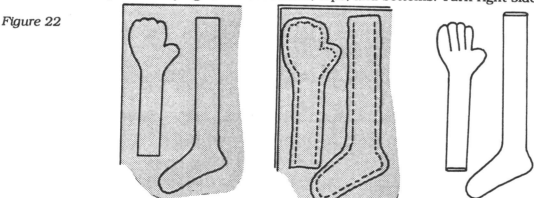

To sew together two parts of a person, press under 1/4" of the end of one piece. Place the end of the adjoining piece into it -- up to the pattern line -- and slipstitch together. Sew arms to shoulders at a slight angle (Fig. 23).

Figure 23

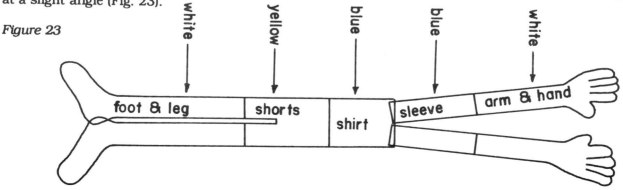

Draw the lines between the fingers with a black laundry marker.

10) Trace seven heads, using the "FULL SIZE HEAD PATTERN" (trace only the outline, not the features) on the wrong side of white satin, leaving at least 1/2" in between heads. Turn the fabric over and trace a different face design inside each head outline on the right side of the fabric using a black laundry marker and the method described in Step 1.

Place fabric with head outlines on top of another piece of white satin -- right sides together -- and stitch head outlines, leaving the necks open for turning. Cut out heads 1/4" from stitching. Turn right side out and press. Fold most of the neck inside; slipstitch opening closed and press. Slipstitch neck into position on shoulders. Tack top of head to arms with a few stitches to keep head from flopping down.

11) Lightly pencil in a hairline (Fig. 24) and add hair as shown with a large hole needle and six-strand embroidery floss of the desired hair color. The floss is knotted at the scalp for the straight hair; it is stitched twice in the same place for short, curly hair. It takes approximately four and one-half skeins of floss to do long hair and bangs on one head. The amount varies with how thick and long you make the hair.

Figure 24

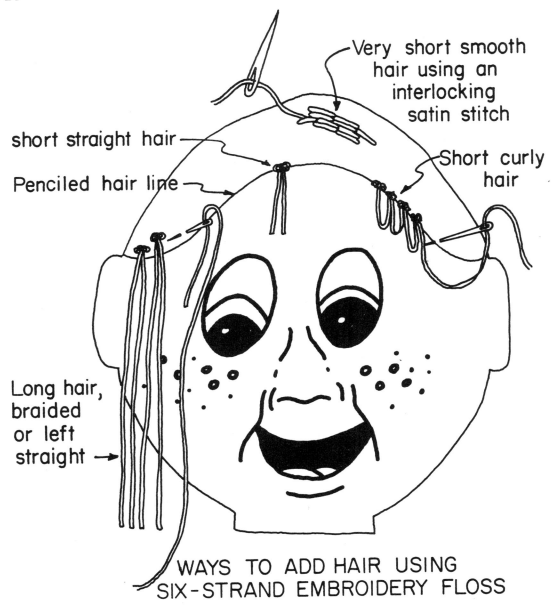

Very short smooth hair using an interlocking satin stitch

short straight hair

Penciled hair line

Short curly hair

Long hair, braided or left straight →

WAYS TO ADD HAIR USING SIX-STRAND EMBROIDERY FLOSS

12) Details such as a string of tiny beads for a necklace or tiny buttons can be added if desired.

13) The last step is to fold the fingers of the people over the lower wood rod and secure with a few stitches. The person with the double circle eyes should be hung upside down.

Figure 25

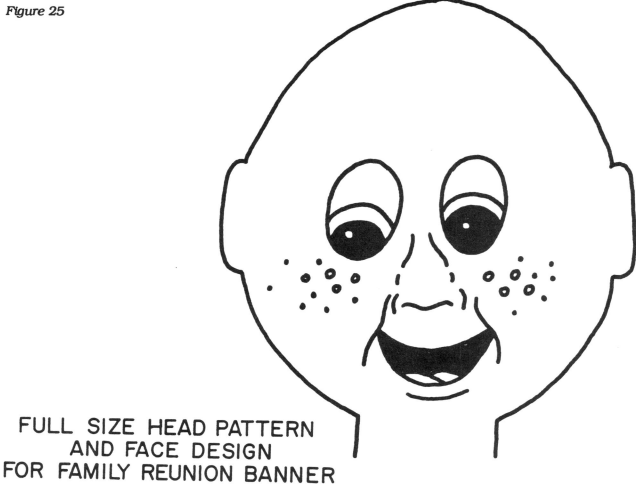

FULL SIZE HEAD PATTERN
AND FACE DESIGN
FOR FAMILY REUNION BANNER

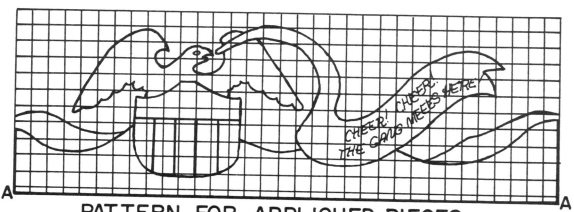

PATTERN FOR APPLIQUED PIECES
ON FAMILY REUNION BANNER
SCALE: 1 SQUARE = 1 INCH

Figure 26

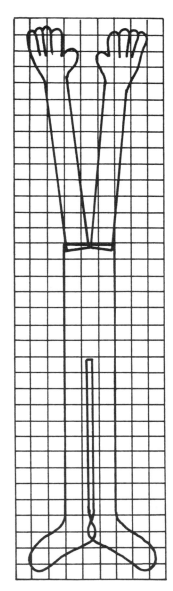

PATTERN FOR PEOPLE ON
FAMILY REUNION BANNER
SCALE: I SQUARE = I INCH

FULL SIZE LETTERING
FOR FAMILY REUNION BANNER

CHEER! CHEER! CHEETS HERE!
THE GANG MEETS HERE!

Figure 27

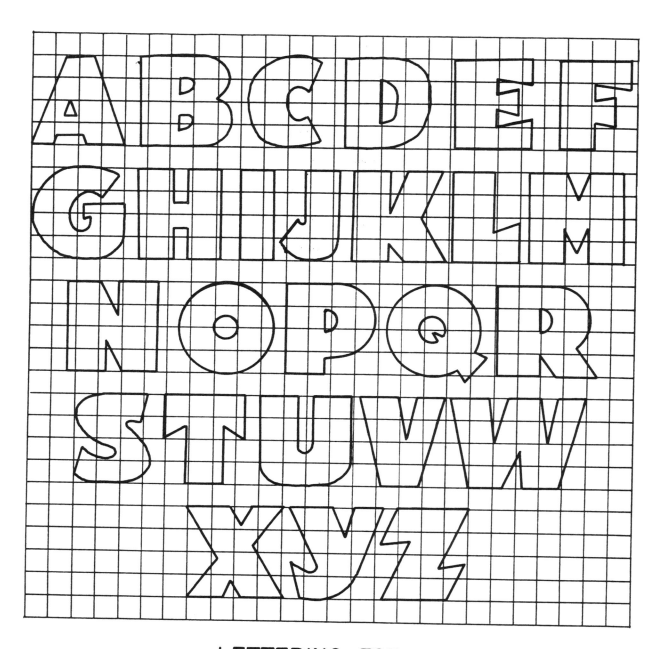

LETTERING FOR
FAMILY REUNION BANNER
SCALE: 1 SQUARE = 1 INCH

Figure 28

FULL SIZE FACE DESIGNS
FOR FAMILY REUNION BANNER

Figure 29

FULL SIZE FACE DESIGNS
FOR FAMILY REUNION BANNER

WIND SOCK

Photo 15

Make several brightly colored wind socks for festive decorations at your outdoor family gatherings. At the close of the reunion you might want to put the names of all children present on folded strips of paper in a hat and hold a drawing to see who gets to take a wind sock home as a memento.

The amount of fabric required depends on how many colors you will be using. One one-color wind sock requires 2/3 yard of 45" wide fabric (with some leftover scrap). Draw the pieces on grid paper of the same width as the fabric to calculate how much of each color of fabric you will need when using more than one color.

MATERIALS NEEDED (per wind sock):

Ripstop nylon (or similar fabric)   Lanyard hook (or 1/2" plastic ring)
Fabric paint   thread
1 yard thin nylon cording   darning needle
16 1/2" of 1/2" wide boning   white glue

INSTRUCTIONS:

1. Cut two 8" x 12" rectangles (for Top) and eight 3" x 26" rectangles (for Streamers). Use fabric paint to decorate with desired designs. Let dry thoroughly.

Figure 30   *Figure 31*

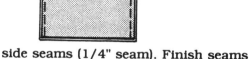

Figure 30

FABRIC KEY
Right side of fabric.
Wrong side of fabric.

2. With right sides together, sew Top rectangles together at side seams (1/4" seam). Finish seams with zig-zag stitch to prevent fraying.

3. To make casing for boning, press 1/4" under along upper edge of Top; press another 3/4" under. Stitch along edge as shown, leaving an opening to insert boning. Insert boning into casing. (Note: it will be easier to push boning through casing if you cover the end with tape first.) Stitch overlapping ends of boning together securely. Stitch opening closed.

Figure 32

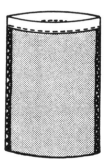

4. To make Streamers, press 1/4" under on three sides of each Streamer; press another 1/4" under. Stitch as shown.

If you want a pointed end on the Streamer, fold one corner on finished end as shown and stitch along side edge.

Figure 33

Figure 34

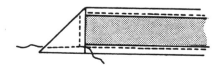

5. With right sides together, pin unfinished ends of streamers to lower edge of Top. Stitch (1/4" seam). Finish seam with zig-zag stitch to prevent fraying. Press seam toward Top. Topstitch as shown.

Figure 35

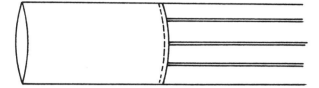

6. Cut three 12" long pieces of cord. Make three dots on the upper brim of the wind sock (just under the boning), dividing it into thirds. Thread each piece of cord through a darning needle and knot one end. Push needle from inside to outside at dot.

Knot the three cords together above windsock and fasten to hook. Apply glue to all knots to keep them from fraying.

Figure 36

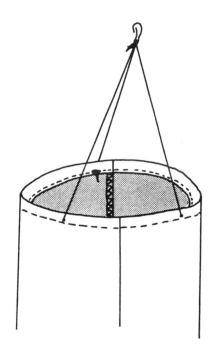

Figure 37. Sample design for wind sock.

Figure 38. Sample alphabet style for wind sock.

DESIGNING A COAT OF ARMS

In the days of old when knights dressed themselves so thoroughly in protective armor that it was hard to tell who was on which side, their shields were used as a means of highly visible identification. The various shape, color, and symbol combinations differentiated one clan from another while also providing some protection during the battles. It eventually became tradition to pass these distinctive designs down in the family from generation to generation, with a small change in design for each person. These designs were known as coats of arms.

Many families have invested a lot of time and money to trace their ancestry back several generations and take great pride in displaying the original coat of arms which was granted to an ancestor in one branch of the family tree many, many years ago. There are also advertisements in various magazines placed by companies who offer to supply you with a coat of arms to match your family surname for a fee. Logic should tell you that for $30 these companies are not tracing your particular lineage to be sure that the Anderson coat of arms design they send you actually belonged to one of your ancestors. Not only that, but what about all the other people with other surnames whose marriages or love affairs through the years eventually resulted in your existence?

Designing your own coat of arms can often be much more meaningful -- and fun! Perhaps you will prefer to call it a family emblem instead of a coat of arms. The design could be printed on stationery used for family reunion correspondence, or on fund-raising or souvenir objects such as cookbooks, T-shirts, embroidered patches, mugs, bookplates, etc.

There are many books written about heraldry and the traditional rules for designing a coat of arms. Check out what is available at your library or bookstore if you wish. One book which is especially informative for the beginner is *The Heraldry Book: A Guide to Designing Your Own Coat of Arms* by Marvin Grosswirth (New York: Doubleday, 1981). You may find the subject so fascinating that you will seek out heraldry courses to take, or you can follow the simplified guidelines given here -- combining some old rules with new ideas to create an emblem which is meaningful to you and pleasing to the eye. It's not that hard. (Note: purists will no doubt consider this whole section blasphemy, but look at it this way: Americans have been improvising and innovating, combining new and old, ever since they started this country! It's worked pretty well so far.)

You will need some tracing paper, which is available at art or drafting supply stores and many office supply stores. Refer to Fig. 39 and Fig. 40 to decide which shield shape you prefer. Place the tracing paper over the design and trace with a pencil. Now you are ready to decide what will go inside and outside this outline, whether it will have a motto, and so on.

The surface of the shield, called the field, can be designed with more than one color. See Fig. 41 for a variety of ways to part the field. These lines of partition can be straight or you can use any of the styles shown in Fig. 42. Pencil in your line(s) of partition, if you choose to use any.

Next, choose the symbols and figures, if any, that you would like to decorate the shield with. These can be purely decorative or can symbolize an idea, thought, motto, or name that has special meaning for your family. You can use plants, animals, heavenly bodies, man-made objects, and human forms as illustrated in Fig. 43 and Fig 44. Use a copy machine or the block by block method to reduce or enlarge the designs as needed. Names and initials can also be used to generate some interesting symbols.

The traditional heraldry colors are red, blue, green, purple, and black. Fig. 45 shows how to denote the colors on the shield according to traditional hatching patterns for black and white drawings of the shield. One old rule when creating a coat of arms is that no metal should be placed on another metal and no color placed on another color.

Most traditional coats of arms have a helmet placed on top of the shield, such as shown in Fig. 46. Use one if you like, but an emblem which will look less medieval and is frequently identified with the United States is the eagle (see Fig. 47 and Fig. 48). An eagle would seem a more appropriate symbol in a peace and freedom loving country such as ours which has been a melting pot for so many nationalities. You could also choose another emblem or none at all. That's the fun of designing your own coat of arms.

Along with a helmet, a mantle is usually included. A mantle was a cloth or cape worn by a knight to protect him from the sun's rays and rain. It is represented on a coat of arms with elaborate twists and curves (Fig. 49) and usually uses the main color and main metal of the shield. A wreath made of two colors of silk (usually the same two colors as the mantle) twisted together was used to attach the mantle to the helmet. If you want to include one, draw it as six twists of silk as shown in Fig. 50.

Another ornamental figure can be drawn on top of the wreath. This is called a crest and can be a plant, animal, human, or any part thereof. Refer to Fig. 43 and Fig. 44 again for ideas on what you might like to use.

Decide whether or not you would like to include a motto. This can be written on a scroll underneath the shield, on top of it, or all around it. A variety of scroll styles are shown in Fig. 51 and Fig. 52. The motto could be a patriotic expression, a battle cry, a moral or religious idea, a hobby or line of work, or a theme of life. You may want to express it in Latin, English, or the language of the country where most of your ancestors came from. Fig. 53 is one style of alphabet that can be used when writing out the motto. Although this would be considered a redundancy by heraldry rules and experts, you may wish to display the family surname below the coat of arms.

Sample Mottos

Always Ready	I Will Not Forget
By Courage and Love	The Victory is in The Trying
God Willing	By Actions Be Ye Judges
Compassion and Courage are All	For Country and Family
Try	Go Boldly With Faith
Speak With Actions	May Truth Conquer
Let God be our Guide	Hold Steadfast to Honor
Come What May	First In Battle
What Will Be Will Be	Break Not the Bond
Trust Wisely	Never By Chance
Truth Conquers	The Honor is in the Attempt
Do Well in All Things	With Solitude Comes Wisdom
The Light in Darkness	With Unity is Success
From Difficulty comes Pleasure	By Wisdom Not Chance
To Breathe is to Hope	Stand Sure
Hold Firm to Beliefs	We Were, Are, and Will Be
Prudence is our Edge	

Many coats of arms also include two figures, such as lions, on either side of the shield holding it up. The figures and the shield are all placed on a small area of ground, and this entire design is called an achievement. In the interest of keeping the emblem small enough so as not to be obnoxious on stationery or other small items, you may prefer to not include the supporting figures or the ground.

You may want to find a heraldry artist who can paint your emblem once you have designed it. Your local historical or genealogical society can probably supply you with a list of local artists capable of such work.

Figure 39. Shield shapes.

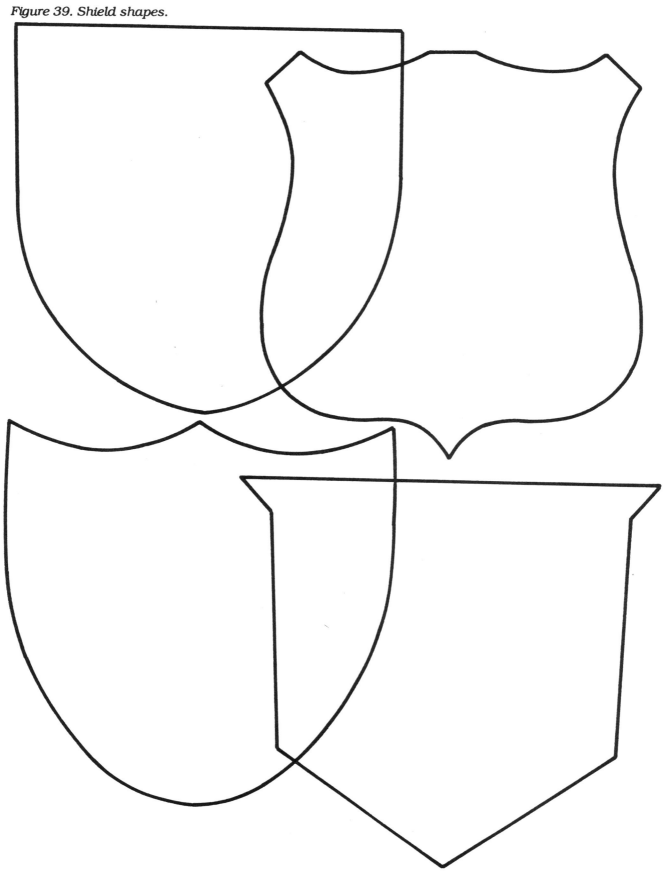

Figure 40. Shield shapes.

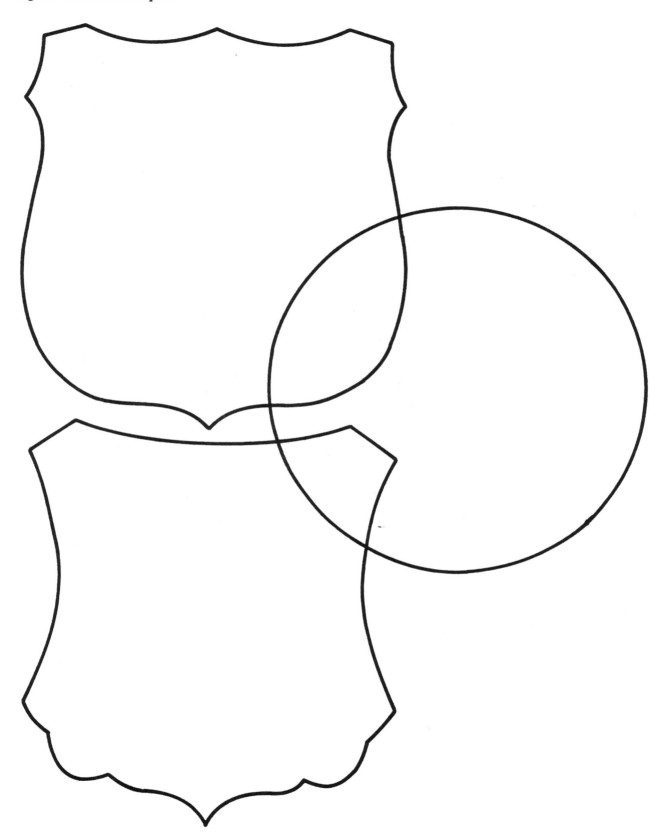

Figure 41. Sample geometric designs and divisions on shields.

Figure 42. Types of lines of partition.

Figure 43. Sample symbols for shields.

Figure 44. Sample symbols for shields.

Figure 45. Traditional color symbols.

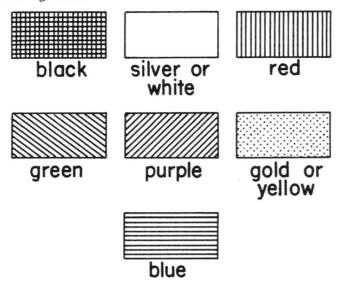

black   silver or white   red

green   purple   gold or yellow

blue

Figure 46.

A fictitious coat of arms with the traditional helmet.

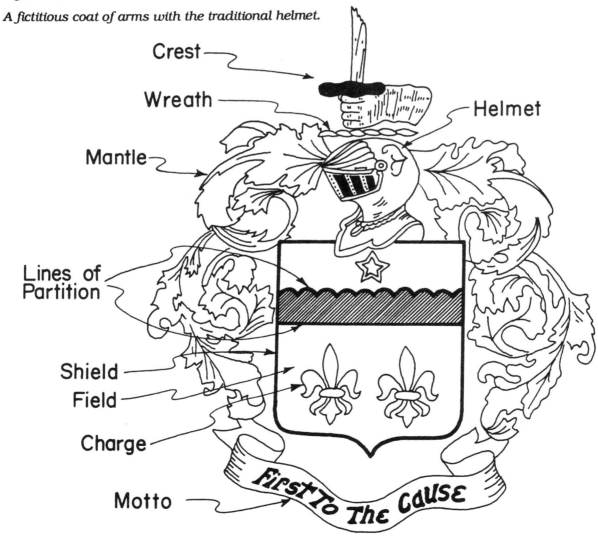

Crest

Wreath

Helmet

Mantle

Lines of Partition

Shield

Field

Charge

Motto

First To The Cause

Figure 47. A fictitious coat of arms using an eagle instead of a helmet.

Figure 48. Sample eagle designs.

Figure 49. Mantle styles. Reverse the design for the opposite side of the shield.

Figure 50. Wreath.

Figure 51. Scroll styles.

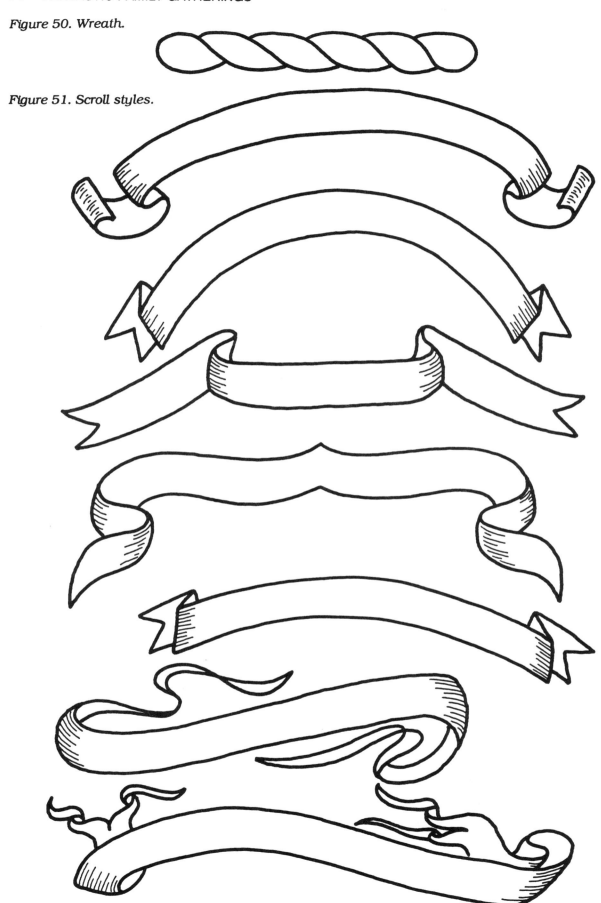

Figure 52. Scroll styles.

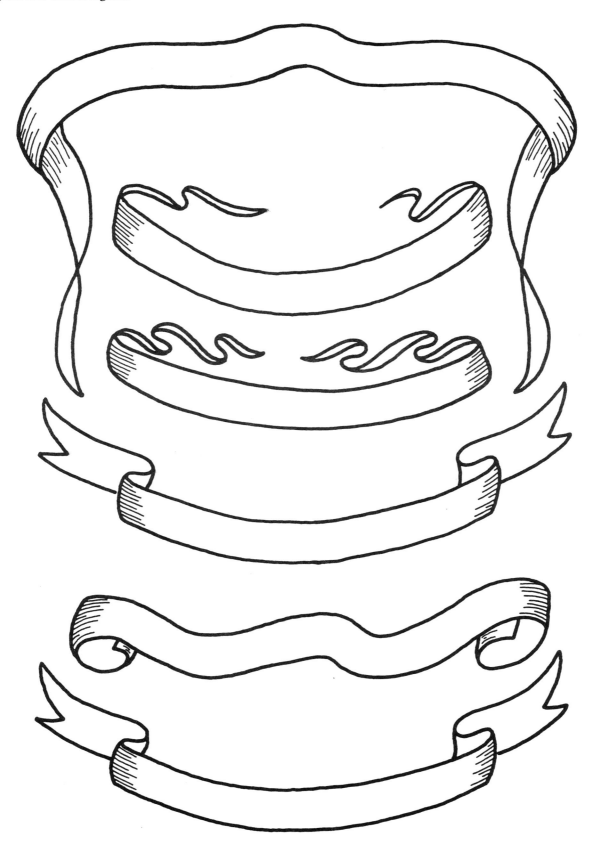

Figure 53. Sample alphabet to use on scrolls.

ABCDEFGHIJKLMNOPQ
STUVWXYZ abcdefghijklmn
opqrstuvwxyz
0123456789

OTHER TYPES OF FAMILY EMBLEMS

A coat of arms isn't your only option for a family emblem. Ellie Anthenat of Illinois designed this symbol for her family (Fig. A). The tepee forms a stylized 'A' -- the first letter of the surname. Seven suns and one moon represent her seven sons and one daughter. There is a flame in the campfire for each of her children's spouses. The 'chips' around the tree stump are the fifteen grandchildren.

Fig. B shows a simplified version of the symbol which was used for embroidered patches handed out at the first Anthenat Reunion.

Figure A

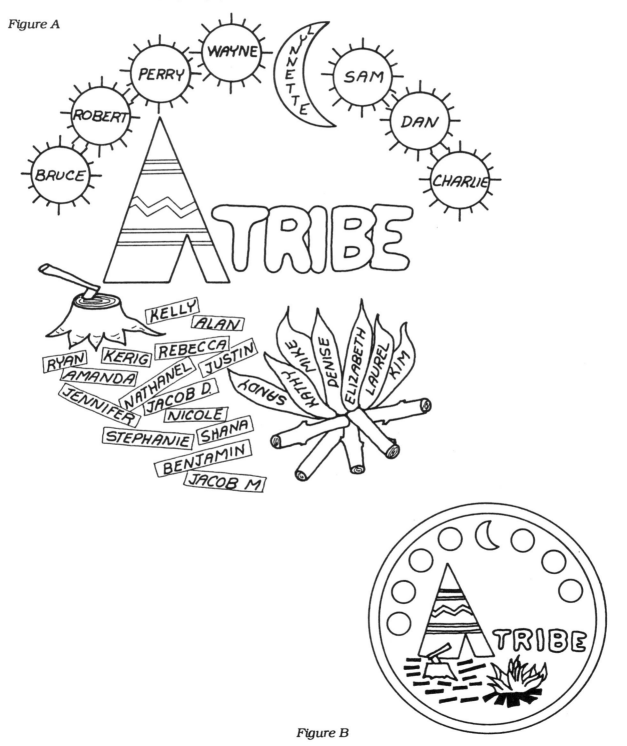

Figure B

SCALE MODEL OF A HOUSE

Photo 16

If you are looking for something that makes a great conversation piece at a family reunion, a unique centerpiece for a table, a wonderful keepsake, or something to sell at a family auction to generate money for future reunions, consider making a scale model of a past or present family home. You might choose the farmhouse that your great-grandfather built from timber cut from the woods around it, or the cottage on the lake. Or instead of a home, you might decide on your grandfather's big red barn or the corner grocery store that another relative owned.

If you feel a little intimidated by the idea of building a scale model, don't be. It's not that hard if you follow the general instructions given here; you will be amazed and proud when it begins to take shape. It's just a matter of patience and working one step at a time. Model houses require more time than money to make, and the work is relaxing and enjoyable. If you add another window or a few more strips of siding every evening while watching your favorite television show it will be done before you know it.

These instructions are for a wood frame house with standard horizontal siding. If the home you want to recreate is made of brick, the same instructions apply until you get to the section on siding. Plastic sheets with a brick pattern are available from hobby stores which carry supplies for model railroads. Cut the sheets to size for the sides, cut out window and door rectangles, and glue in place.

The .25" = 1' scale used here will make the model small enough to fit nicely on a shelf or chest, and large enough to be able to include details such as window trim and roof shingles. Also, if displaying a Lionel 027 train set under the Christmas tree is a tradition in your home, constructing the model to this scale will give you another building of the proper size for your display.

Photo 17: This scene includes models of the houses of three sets of grandparents and a model of the children's play house. A small sign identifies each structure.

MATERIALS NEEDED:

Photographs of the house	single pane clear acrylic sheet
Graph paper	Medium grit sandpaper
1/4" thick wood	White glue
1/16" x 1/8" balsa trim	Hot glue gun
1/8" thick balsa	Paint
1/64" thick birch	

INSTRUCTIONS:

Photographs.

First, take photographs of each side of the house. When doing this, stand in the middle of the side and just far enough away from the house to get the whole side in the photograph. The larger the side is in the photograph, the easier it will be to estimate window measurements and other details later when making your scale drawings.

If you want to make a model of a house which no longer exists, collect what photographs you can of the structure. Borrow photos from relatives and use your best guess for what you don't have photographs to show. An uncle who once helped shingle it might remember the overall size and shape of the roof. Another person might remember that there were three little windows on one side of the building because as a child she thought they looked like a cat's eyes and nose. Ask around and jog some memories. You might want to use one family gathering to find out about the house, and then build it before the next reunion; it will give everyone another reason to look forward to the next reunion!

Sometimes a photo of the front of the house can be readily found, but the sides and back are another matter. In the past when family photos were taken the people often stood against the side of the house in order to have a solid color background for the group photo. Examine the backgrounds in your family photos.

Measurements.

At the minimum you will need the total length and height of each outer wall. Beyond this, it's up to you how many additional measurements you want to take. The more measurements you take the more accurate your model will be, but you can do a good job of estimating many of them from the photographs if you have the overall dimensions of a wall and you were at the center of that wall when you took the photograph. Measure the width of the siding and the height of the foundation. Later, using the photographs, you can calculate how far the windows are from the ground by counting the number of rows of siding underneath them and multiplying by the width of a single row. The same applies to the height of the roof peak.

If the house no longer exists, you still have ways of approximating the measurements. Some dimensions on houses are fairly standard, such as the height of a front door. Measure your own front door. Is the height of the house in the photo three times the height of its front door? Multiply the height of your front door by three and you have the approximate height of the house. Use the same method for width.

Scale Drawings.

Next, draw a floor plan to scale for the outside walls (Fig. 54) using grid paper and the overall outside wall measurements that you took. Remember that the scale you are using is .25" = 1' which means that 1/4" on the paper represents one foot on the actual house. Therefore, if the front of the house actually measured 26', you would measure 6.5" on the grid paper (.25 x 26 = 6.5).

Draw a side view for each side of the house (Fig. 55). It will be easier if you make a special ruler on the edge of an index card for each photograph. For instance, if the 26' wide front of the house is actually 2.7" in the photograph, make a mark for zero near the corner of the index card, and make another mark 2.7" down from the zero. Label this second mark 26'. In exactly the center of these two marks, make another mark and label it 13'. A mark in the middle between 0' and 13' would be 7.5', and so on.

Figure 54

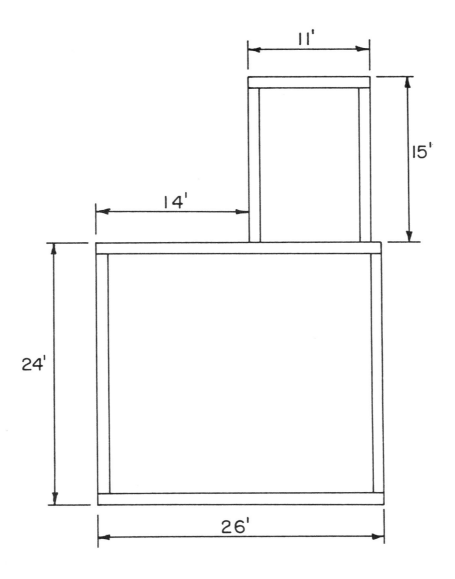

Figure 55

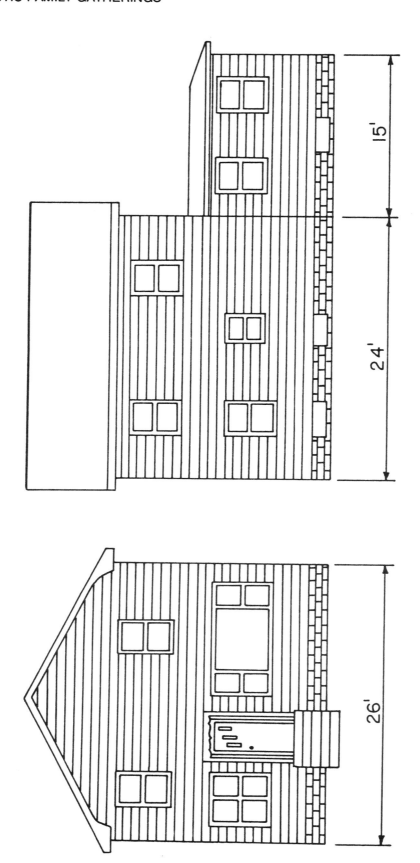

You can now use this index-card ruler to measure distances in that particular photograph. Multiply the foot measurement by .25 to get the number of inches to measure on your grid paper. Don't worry, it's not as difficult as it sounds! Remember to count the number of rows of siding as a double check on how high the windows and roof go. As you draw, trust your eyes. If it looks right to your eyes, it's accurate enough.

Cutting Out Wood Sides and Roof.

From the side-view drawings make patterns for cutting out the sides and roof of the house (Fig. 56). Be sure to allow for the thickness of the wood when drawing patterns for two pieces which meet at a corner. Use front and side drawings together to get roof pattern dimensions.

Figure 56

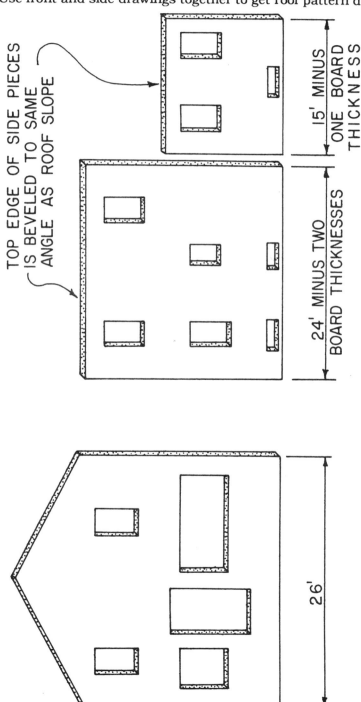

Trace the pattern onto 1/4" thick wood and cut out. You can drill a large hole into the center of each window for a place to get a jigsaw started. Sand all edges smooth.

Bevel the edges that form the peak of the roof to get a tight fit. Pencil on guidelines for the shingles now -- before assembling the wood pieces. Draw them .2" apart. Always start at the bottom edge of the roof piece and measure up. Also, pencil on guidelines for the siding strips on the sides (Fig. 57); these are also .2" apart. Start at the foundation line and measure up. Before you begin gluing the parts together you might want to cover the interior side of the walls with scraps of wallpaper (with a very small design) or paint them.

Figure 57

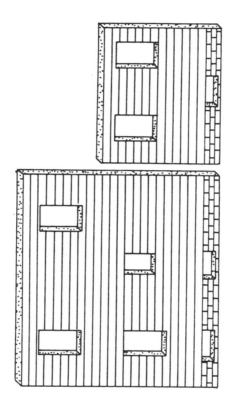

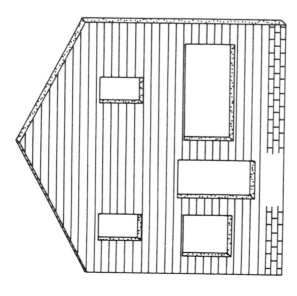

Windows and Doors.

Tape the original side-view drawings to a flat surface. Tape waxed paper on top of them, and construct the window and door trim on top of the drawings with 1/16" x 1/8" balsa trim (available at hobby stores). The 1/8" is actually wider than it should be for this scale but the extra width here is more pleasing to the eye. Make miter joints with a razor blade and glue together on the wax paper. When dry, glue the trim onto the house in the proper locations. Paint the trim and the raw edges of the window and door openings the appropriate color.

Cover single-pane clear acrylic (such as Plexiglas) with clear contact paper to protect it from scratches. Draw on the required sizes of window panes. Cut out the window panes with a fine tooth blade and remove the contact paper. Cover the edges with glue and insert in place.

To finish the inside walls, cut one-piece window trims and door trims from unruled index cards and glue in place. Cut doors from 1/8" balsa wood. Raised panels in the doors can be cut from 1/64" birch and glued on balsa wood bases. For door knobs, glue on small size shot.

Assembly and Details.

To assure squared-up corners, cover the outside-wall floor plan drawing with waxed paper and assemble the structure on top of it. A hot glue gun will make faster and stronger joints, but any wood glue can be used. You can use sandpaper or spackling compound to sand off bumps or fill in gaps in the glued joints. Glue the roof on last.

Front steps can be made from 1/8" thick balsa rectangles, gluing together as many rectangles as needed to obtain the needed step height and sanding the edges smooth. Paint the foundation and steps a brownish-gray color.

Siding.

Cut 1/4" wide strips from 1/64" thick birch for the siding, using scissors and cutting slowly with the grain. Lay the strips on wax paper and paint one side the desired color. Let dry; trim to the proper length and angle -- one at a time -- with a razor blade, and glue onto the house. Start at the bottom and install that row of siding all the way around the house before beginning the next higher row.

Roofing.

Cut medium-grit sandpaper into 1/4" wide strips for roof shingles. Every 1/2" on each strip, cut a thin notch with scissors -- half the width of the strip. (Tip: draw all of these cutting lines in pencil on the reverse side of sandpaper before you begin cutting). Glue the shingle strips to the roof one at a time, starting at the bottom edge. Alternate the notches to make a typical roofing pattern. Glue un-notched strips on the peaks. If the sandpaper starts to buckle up as it is drying, press it with the palm of your hand briefly. The pressure and your body heat will make the shingles lay down smooth again while they dry.

Additional Comments and Suggestions.

1. Don't let the amount of instructions here discourage you. Just take it one step at a time and go slow. Patience is the key word. The finished product is well worth the time and effort, and it will be a heirloom to pass down from generation to generation.

2. If the house has a block foundation, use an engraver or the sharp point of a nut picker to make grooves in the wood for individual blocks. Do this after the sides have been glued together so that the corner blocks will match up properly.

3. Consider making a number of these models -- perhaps one per year -- for a truly special center-piece at reunions. As time and money permit, add accessories to the scene that can be made or bought from hobby stores. Use some twigs to make fences like the ones at Grandpa Smith's farm. Make a row of tiny red geraniums like the ones Grandpa Ruple always plants in front of his house. Stick a small branch tip in a mound of plaster of Paris and construct a crude mini-treehouse that resembles the one you made as a kid in the maple tree in the back yard.

4. You can buy small evergreens from hobby and craft stores to landscape the scale model with, but usually the little wood bases on them are so small that the trees keep toppling over. Buy large

heavy washers from the hardware store, put a small mound of wet plaster of Paris on a washer, and push the base of the tree down in it. When the new base is dry you can paint it green if you are planning a summer scene or white for a snow scene.

6. If the base of the house is left open, you can place a miniature electric Christmas tree (sold in dollhouse supply stores) inside and light it up for a particularly beautiful effect at night.

ADDRESSES OF COMPANIES OFFERING PRODUCTS
SUITABLE FOR REUNION MEMENTOS, AWARDS, DECORATIONS:

1. Dinn Bros., Inc.
   68 Winter Street
   P.O. Box 111
   Holyoke, MA 01041-0111
       (800) 628-9657
       FAX 800-876-7497
   (trophies, medals, award ribbons, engraved trays and tankards,
   pen sets, plaques, gavels, certificates, etc.)

2. Marquis Awards & Specialties, Inc.
   108 N. Bent Street
   Powell, WY 82435
       (307) 754-2272
       (800) 327-2446
       FAX 307-754-9577
   (pens, flying discs, mugs, letter openers, medals, ribbons, plaques, trophies, buttons,
   identification badges, embroidered patches, cloisonne lapel pins, decals,
   bumper stickers, banners, certificates, clothing, etc.

3. The Patch Works
   P.O. Box 2696
   Louisville, KY 40201
       (800) 634-0164
       FAX 800-497-7844
   (embroidered patches, enameled emblems, vinyl decals, coffee mugs, etc.)

4. PDF, Inc.
   Dept. FR
   5934 Woodridge Hill
   San Antonio, TX 78249
       (512) 561-0685
       (800) 551-0346
   (shirts, jackets, caps, bumper stickers, tote bags, embroidered patches, crest pins,
   commemorative tiles with your coat of arms or reunion design, mugs, etc.)

5. The Queensboro Shirt Company
   119 N. 11th Street
   Greenpoint, NY 11211
       (800) 847-4478
   (custom shirts, tote bags, caps)

6. Reunion Specialties Company
   11 Browning Street
   Riverside, CA 92507
       (714) 276-4944
       (800) 472-4550

(invitations, balloons, pens, banners, porcelain cups, post cards to be used as reminders, ribbons, rosettes, certificates, buttons, medallions, award pins, plaques, tote bags, hats, shirts, jackets, etc.)

7. We Love Country
   100 E. Sedgwick Street
   Philadelphia, PA 19119
       (800) 322-3034
       FAX 215-849-6231
   (You can commission custom designed afghans which feature photos, artwork, etc.)

8. West Tape & Label, Inc.
   3845 Forest Street
   Denver, CO 80207
       (800) 255-7314
       (303) 388-5821
       FAX 303-321-4536
   (pressure-sensitive labels of all shapes and sizes)

9. Erie Landmark Company
   4449 Brookfield Corporate Drive
   Chantilly, VA 22021-1681
       (800) 874-7848
       FAX 703-818-2157
   (plaques, time capsules)

10. Historical Research Center
    922 Zeletta Drive
    Akron, OH 44319
        (216) 644-3888
    (coat of arms plaques, pendants, mugs)

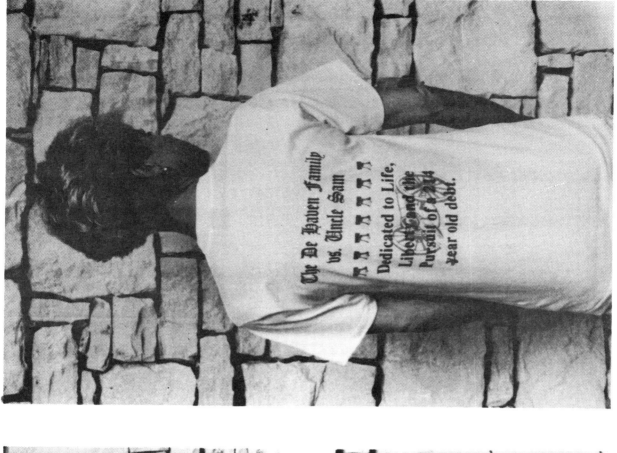

Photos 18 and 19: Courtesy of Pat Fitzgerald. PDF, Inc. custom printed special t-shirts for the DeHaven Reunion. The message "The DeHaven Family vs Uncle Sam. Dedicated to Life, Liberty, and the Pursuit of a 214 year old debt" refers to an unsettled debt between ancestor Jacob DeHaven and the U.S. government. In 1777 Jacob loaned approximately $450,000 in gold and supplies to the U.S. to aid in the American Revolution. The promissory note from the government was never paid off.

Fundraising Ideas

Handling the cost of a family reunion can be a touchy balancing act; you don't want one person to get stuck paying for a lot of the expenses but you also don't want to end up charging a per person fee that will prevent some relatives on tight budgets from attending. One solution is the pass-the-hat approach; supply a box with a slot in the lid or a basket and ask for voluntary donations. Whether a person slips in a $1 bill or a $20 bill is up to them.

Another solution is to hold group fundraisers during the reunion. The relatives at the Lemaster/Patterson Reunion raise money for reunion expenses by holding a White Elephant Auction every year:

"It is the big highlight of our reunion," says Phyllis Rhodes of New Mexico. "One of our cousins is a professional auctioneer and he does the auction for us. We all enjoy the auction and buy stuff at outrageous prices because we know the money is going for a good cause. We use the money to supplement the cost of our newsletter and cover the costs of our next reunion. We raise $200-250 each time."

If you would like to hold an auction at your reunion, be sure to inform everyone when you send out information about the reunion six months in advance, and again when reminder notices are sent out. Ask each family to donate a new or used article(s) for the White Elephant table. The idea is to make money and have fun doing it. Laughter inevitably breaks out when the same strange looking whatchamacallit that was on the table last year ends up on the table again this year!

Photo 20: Courtesy of Fern Hill. The auctioneer takes a bid at the Lemaster/Patterson Reunion.

Plan a specific time for the auction to begin. JoAnne McIntyre of West Virginia says that the Hamrick Clan craft auction usually starts around three in the afternoon:

"Everyone who can brings something nice they have made, such as quilts, pillows, painted sweatshirts, padded albums, old family photographs specially framed, etc."

JoAnne is an artist and her contribution is usually a painted scene from her grandparents' farm, some of which have added $150 to $200 to the family coffers. One year she made a padded album containing stories she had collected during the year from her grandparents' children -- her aunts and uncles:

Photo 21: Courtesy of Wanda Copeland. Family members share something of themselves with each other: a carved little man sitting on a bench whittling a chain, a carved cow, a wall hanging, etc.

"They were things they remembered while growing up and they were priceless," she says. The album went for $200. "Kinfolk were bidding against each other for treasures to take home, knowing that it would help make next year's reunion a success!"

Often there is a member of the family who specializes in creating certain handmade items for the auction and everyone looks forward to seeing what he or she has created this year. Joy Whitenack of Arkansas says that one 86-year-old cousin usually crochets a tablecloth or makes a quilt for her contribution to the Robinett Family Reunion auction.

In one family a will was responsible for the first family auction. The grandfather left instructions in his will that at the first family reunion following his death all sentimental keepsakes and valuable heirlooms that he owned should be auctioned off to family members only. He wanted the items to be kept in the family and the money generated to be put in a bank account to be used solely for the purpose of paying for family reunions long after he was gone.

According to Roberta Mingyar of West Virginia the first auction for the Himes-Schaffer Family Reunion was held when her Grandmother Shaffer died: "Several articles of clothing which belonged to my great grandmother had been kept through the years by my grandmother. When she died my uncle wanted to be fair and offer everyone in our family an opportunity to have one of these keepsakes. Thus the idea of an auction and he would not be playing 'favorites'. Everyone was happy with the results. All the money from the auction was deposited in the reunion bank account by the treasurer."

The Bock family adds a surprise element to their auctions. Everyone is asked to bring a small, inexpensive gift -- either wrapped or in a bag -- and to write on it whether it is for an adult or child. They have found that wrapped gifts usually bring in more money than unwrapped ones.

"We have had some gag gifts in the past years, such as when someone bought a rock, but everyone has taken them in stride and not complained," says family member Sonia Cesarino of Pennsylvania. "During the last reunion we had a 30-second limit for bidding, which certainly livened up the bidding."

This family also used other methods for raising money to pay for their reunions. For the last three years they have held a 50-50 Raffle. "We sell tickets and during the auction someone pulls a ticket from the bag," says Sonia. "The winner and the reunion fund halve the proceeds." The ticket are sold for 50 cents each and people usually buy four.

Other families use raffles instead of auctions to raise money for the reunion treasury. Brenda Gotensky of Michigan reports that chances were sold on two handmade afghans to help pay for the food and drinks at their party. Jo Ann Casebier of Kansas reports that each of the six original families in the Colburn Reunion is responsible for bringing a large item (large stained glass window, afghan, etc.) for a raffle at their family reunion.

Photo 22: To create a special sweatshirt like this for the family auction take a favorite photo (perhaps your great-grandparents' wedding photo) to a printing shop and have an iron-on transfer made from it. (It can be enlarged at the same time if you wish.) Use puff-up fabric paint to write the name and year of the reunion on the sweatshirt. Ask everyone to sign it with a laundry marker before auction time.

Paintings and drawings are always popular at family auctions and raffles, especially when the subject matter relates to the family or their heritage. If someone in the family paints or draws -- even if they are only just beginning to develop their skill such as a teenager in a high school art class -- ask them to put their talents to work to create something for the family auction. It could be an ink drawing of the store that a great-grandfather once owned, the barn on a family farm, a portrait of a living or dead relative, or a still-life of a couple of keepsake items on a table. A person with a talent for needlework could create a fabric 'painting' of Grandma hanging the wash on the clothesline. Be sure the artist signs the work.

There are also many other ways to raise money as a group for the family treasury. Milton Autry of Alabama reports that some of the ladies in the Autry Family Association ran a refreshment concession (soft drinks, sandwiches, pies, cake, coffee) at a large auction to raise money. Many families produce a video at one reunion and sell copies at next year's gathering. Another idea is to combine fun and profit by having the teens in the family make taffy; making it gives the cousins something enjoyable to do together, and little bags of the finished product can be sold to the rest of the family to munch on during their journey home.

Professionally printed souvenirs such as pencils, mugs, golf caps, and t-shirts with the family name, logo, and year could also be sold. Henrietta Evans of Ohio reports that her family had a special plate with the family tree made for the 100th reunion. Stationery with the family crest is sold by many families. Orders could be taken for copies of old family photos. Be sure to add the cost of postage and mailing envelopes to the price if the items will be mailed.

Use your imagination and brainstorm with other members of your family for ideas. Here are some additional ideas for items to sell, raffle, or auction:

PHOTO CUBE PUZZLES

Photo 23

These charming and unusual puzzles will appeal to friends and family of all ages. No one can resist fiddling with the cubes until they have them correctly assembled to form a picture, and as soon as that person is done someone else will no doubt be waiting to reassemble them into another picture. Once you see how easy they are to make you will be making several of them for door prizes, auction items, etc.

Cubes have six sides, allowing six photos to be used for six different puzzles. You might want use a variety of types of photos for each puzzle or have a theme to the set, such as:
1. six photos from the last reunion
2. six photos of relatives (living or dead) in their military uniforms.
3. six photos about the life of your immigrant ancestor
4. six close-up photos of relatives with pretty smiles on their faces
5. six photos of family heirlooms (with an attached note explaining the significance of each item to the family and who has possession of it.

MATERIALS NEEDED:
   1 1/4" or 1 1/2" wood cubes (available at craft stores)
   6 photographs
   stiff clear plastic (such as a report cover)
   rubber cement
   needle
   scissors

INSTRUCTIONS:
1. Sand the wood cubes smooth. The number of cubes you will need depends on the size of your photographs are. Four cubes will work for standard size snapshots. Using larger photos (5x7 or 8x10) and more cubes will make the puzzle harder and more fun to work!

2. On a piece of graph paper, lay out squares the same size as the cubes and in the formation which will be used (for instance, 2 squares across by 2 squares down or 3 squares across by 4 squares down). Tape a clear plastic sheet over the squares and use a needle to punch a hole at each corner. This will be your see-through template for marking squares on the photographs.

3. Place the template over one photograph, positioning it as desired. Try to avoid things like having a line running through someone's eye. Use a needle to prick a small hole in the photograph at each template hole to mark the corners of the squares. Remove the plastic sheet. Use a straightedge and the needle to carefully scratch connecting lines between the corner holes. Repeat with the remaining five photographs.

4. Use scissors to cut apart the squares on one photo. Mount each photo square on a cube -- one per cube -- using rubber cement. Let dry. Mix up the cubes, ending up with a bare wood side facing upwards on each cube. Cut another photo into squares. Repeat the process until all photos have been mounted. Note: if the cubes aren't quite perfect cubes and the photo hangs over the edge a little on one side, center the photo square on the cube and use a sharp razor blade to trim off any overhang after the rubber cement is dry.

5. The photo cube puzzle can be displayed as is -- either laying down or stacked -- or you can make a tray to hold the cubes. Use thin wood for a base and trim the edges with decorative molding to form a rim. The inner dimensions of the tray should be slightly larger than the assembled cubes. A nice added touch would be to decoupage onto the bottom of the tray a written or typed description of each of the six pictures. Don't forget to add your own signature (as the creator of this delightful conversation piece) and the date.

KEEPSAKE DOLLS

A member of the family who is skilled in doll making might want to create a doll which looks like (or is dressed like) an ancestor. The doll's body could be cloth, papier-maché, ceramic, wood, or any number of other materials. Try to duplicate the clothing in an old family photo. Go to the library and find books on costuming dolls; many have actual patterns which can be enlarged or reduced to match the size of your doll.

One special doll which makes a great conversation piece and fundraising item or door prize is the Heirloom Doll. It will become a treasured keepsake for two reasons: first, the fabric from which each piece of clothing is cut will have a special significance for the family; and second, there is little zipper in the back of the doll's body which opens a secret compartment in the torso. The compartment is large enough to store a variety of things -- a baby shoe, a handkerchief, a letter from a grandfather, etc. If you plan to auction off the doll to raise money, you might not want to divulge what is inside. Let the winning bidder buy a surprise along with the beautiful doll!

Photo 24: The Heirloom Doll on the left has been made according to the instructions given here.
The barefoot doll on the right includes several variations: short sleeve dress, real hair,
and two coats of varnish applied to the head, arms, and legs."

This is a great way to make use of all those sentimental pieces of fabric items which you and your relatives have kept but don't know what to do with. Cut the dress for the doll from the skirt of your great grandmother's dress which was saved to use someday in a patchwork quilt that no one ever seems to have time to start. Remember the beautiful embroidered dresser scarf which was made by your grandmother but unfortunately now has a big perfume stain in the middle? Turn the un-stained ends into a pinafore. Use a lovely piece of tatting made by a great aunt for the edging of the doll's slip. If it's just a tiny piece of tatting or lace use it to trim a pocket on the pinafore or dress. Go through your old trunks, closets, and attic and ask your relatives to do the same. Turn those scraps into a treasured heirloom to be cherished.

If you have a large reunion and need a lot of door prizes or items to be auctioned consider joining forces with a couple of other relatives who enjoy sewing and make four or five dolls, each one featuring different sources for the cloth and trim and something different tucked inside the secret compartment. Perhaps one person could make all the bodies, another the clothes, and yet another the hair and boots.

Be sure to include with each doll a list of what was used to make it. Example:

> This Anderson Heirloom Doll was sewn by ROBERTA T. ANDERSON, CHRISTINA J. BROWN, and FLORA Y. ANDERSON in 1993.
>
> The dress was made from a favorite shirt of Grampa SAM H. ANDERSON. The patched rip you see on the back of the dress skirt was from the time Grampa stood up too fast and caught the back of this shirt on a barb wire fence; he had just been informed that he was going to become a grampa for the first time! The buttons on the dress were handmade from modeling clay by ELIZABETH S. WILLIAMS.
>
> The slip was made from a piece of the bridal veil which Great Grandma BATHSHEBA M. SMITH ANDERSON wore on her wedding day.
>
> The pantaloons were made from a piece of fine linen brought to America by great great grandmother MARY ANDERSON when she came to the U.S. from England. They are trimmed with crocheted lace made by LORI ANDERSON EVANS.
>
> The pinafore is made from a feed sack from back in the days when feed sacks were made with print fabric so farm wives could use them for sewing. Aunt GRACE MILLER added the decorative embroidered initial on the bib.
>
> The shoes were made from vinyl which once covered the seats on Uncle LOUIE G. ANDERSON's much used and loved fishing boat! The tiny buttons on them are actually beads from a necklace belonging to Aunt MARIE H. ANDERSON.
>
> Inside the doll's secret compartment is a lace handkerchief which belonged to Grandma LUCILLE F. ANDERSON, and a letter from her to future generations of the Anderson clan.

HEIRLOOM DOLL INSTRUCTIONS:

Begin by enlarging all pattern pieces (Fig. 70) to full size: 1 square = 1 inch. You will need 1 yard of unbleached muslin, stuffing, embroidery floss, and a 4" zipper for the body; fabric, lace (optional), 1 yard of ribbon, 1/4" wide elastic, and snaps or buttons for the clothes; small buttons and vinyl, felt, or leather for the shoes.

All seams are 1/4" unless otherwise noted.

Figure 58

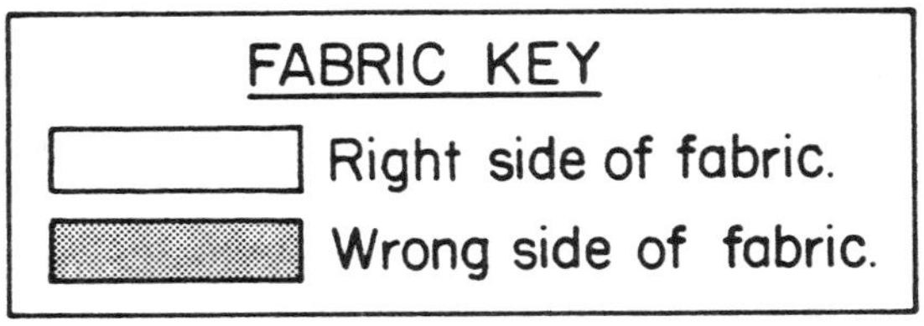

FABRIC KEY

Right side of fabric.

Wrong side of fabric.

Body:
1. Cut from unbleached muslin:
   - 1 Body Back and 1 opposite Body Back
   - 1 Body Front (on fold)
   - 2 Body Arms and 2 opposite Body Arms
   - 2 Body Legs and
   - 2 opposite Body Legs
   - 2 Feet
   - 1 Head Back and 1 opposite Head Back
   - 1 Head Front (embroider features before cutting)
   - 1 Body Front Lining
   - 1 Body Back Lining and 1 opposite Body Back Lining

2. Sew the two Body Back pieces together at center seam (1/2" seam), leaving an area open in the middle for the zipper. (Bottom of zipper should be 1 1/2" up from bottom of fabric.) Press seam

open. Repeat with the two Body Back Lining pieces. Pin zipper in place carefully between the Body Back and the Body Back Lining, wrong sides together, and sew in zipper. Make sure the zipper pull tab will be on the outside of the body.

Figure 59

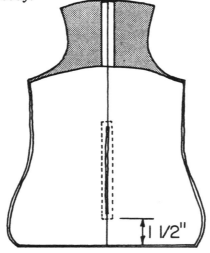

3. Sew Body Front Lining to Body Back Lining all the way around, right sides together. This is the completed secret compartment.

4. Sew Body Back to Body Front at shoulder/neck seams, right sides together. Be careful that you don't catch the lining in this seam. Turn right side out. Fold neck down to dotted line shown on pattern. Set aside.

5. Sew the two Head Back pieces together at center seam, right sides together. Sew Head Back to Head Front, right sides together, leaving neck open. Sew head to neck at folded line. The center seam of the Head Back should be in line with the zipper on the Body Back. Turn right side out. Stuff head and neck very firmly. Sew the base of the neck (the part which had been folded down) closed. Apply blush to doll's cheeks.

Figure 60

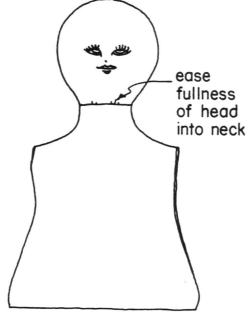

ease fullness of head into neck

Figure 61

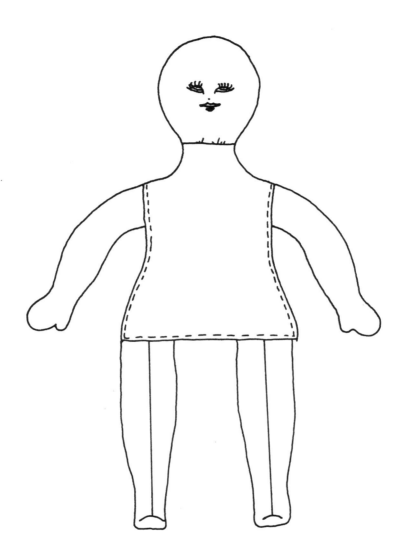

6. Sew two Arm pieces together, right sides together, leaving shoulder end open for turning. Turn right side out and stuff very firmly to 1" from end. Repeat with remaining Arm pieces.

7. Sew two Leg pieces together, leaving both ends open. Sew Foot to foot end of Leg. Turn right side out. Stuff very firmly to 1" from end. Repeat with other two pieces.

8. Press 1/2" under all around on sides and bottom of back and front of torso. Position arms and legs as shown and topstitch sides and bottom (twice for extra strength). Be sure you do not catch any of the lining in the seam.

Figure 62

9. Pencil a hairline on the head as shown. Using embroidery floss of the desired color, make the hair by inserting a needle threaded with six strands in the scalp and back out again for a 1/16" wide stitch. Pull thread to desired hair length. Cut the doubled floss and tie in a double knot at the scalp. Repeat every 1/4" until the hairline and area inside are covered. Style as desired.

USING REAL HAIR ON YOUR HEIRLOOM DOLL

If you decide to make an Heirloom Doll for a daughter or granddaughter you can save the clippings the next time she gets her hair cut and use them for the doll's hair. The clippings should be at least three inches long. Place the cut ends in a thin layer along a piece of bias tape (cut ends of hair in the center). Use a sewing machine and small stitches to sew hair to tape. Fold bias tape over to cover cut ends and stitch again along both edges.

Position hair in layers on the doll's scalp, cutting bias tape to required lengths; sew bias tape to scalp by hand. If you do not have enough hair to completely cover the scalp, use what you have around the edges and fashion a bonnet to cover the rest. Sew the bonnet permanently to the head.

Note: You might want to paint the scalp area with thinned-down fabric paint of the same color as the hair before attaching the hair. Be sure the paint is not too thick or it will be difficult to push a needle through.

Also, for a different look you might consider using a special finish on the head, arms, and legs. You could use several coats of varnish, polyurethane, or any of the porcelain-type finishes found in craft stores. Make a tiny stuffed muslin pillow to try them out on first to decide whether you like the effect. Do not use these finishes on the scalp area of the head; it would be too hard to push a needle through.

Pantaloons.
1. Cut 2 Pantaloon pieces on fold from desired fabric.

Figure 63

2. With right sides together, sew front center seam and back center seam. Press seams open. Press under 1/2" along waistline, then 3/4" to make a casing for 1/4" wide elastic. Topstitch along each edge of casing as shown, leaving an opening for inserting elastic. Measure required elastic for a snug fit on doll (with secret compartment stuffed full of rags). Insert elastic in casing, sew overlapping ends together securely, and stitch opening closed.

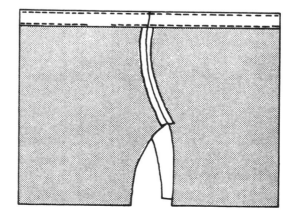

3. Hem bottoms of pantaloons. Add 1 1/2" to 2" wide lace on the bottoms. With right sides together, sew inner leg seam. Turn right side out.

Slip.
1. Cut: 1 Slip Front (on fold)
   1 Slip Back and 1 opposite Slip Back
   two rectangles 10" x 20".

2. With right sides together, sew the two rectangles together as shown.

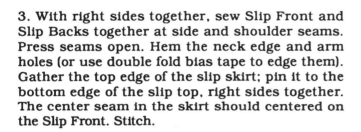

Figure 64

leave 4" open on back center seam.

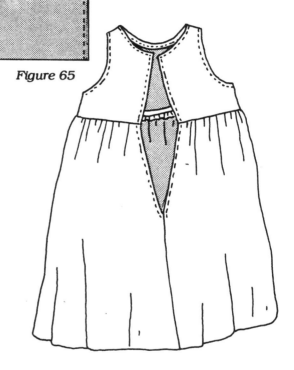

Figure 65

3. With right sides together, sew Slip Front and Slip Backs together at side and shoulder seams. Press seams open. Hem the neck edge and arm holes (or use double fold bias tape to edge them). Gather the top edge of the slip skirt; pin it to the bottom edge of the slip top, right sides together. The center seam in the skirt should centered on the Slip Front. Stitch.

4. Hem the edges of the back opening and use small buttons or snaps to close it. Hem the bottom edge of the slip. Add trim if desired.

Dress.
1. Cut: 1 Dress Front (on fold)
   1 Dress Back and 1 opposite Dress Back
   2 Dress Sleeves (on fold)
   two 11" x 22" rectangles

2. Make a casing for 1/4" elastic in the wrist end of each sleeve by pressing under 1/4" and then 1/2". Topstitch next to edge as shown. Measure doll's wrist for length of elastic required, adding extra for seam. Insert elastic in casing and secure ends with a couple of stitches.

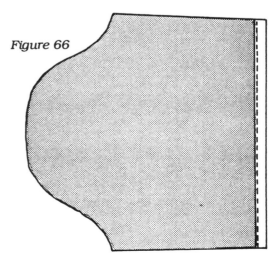

Figure 66

3. With right sides together, sew Dress Front to the two Dress Back pieces at shoulders. Press seam open. Gather the edge of the sleeve from "x" to "x" and pin sleeve to arm opening in the dress top, right sides together. Stitch. Sew underarm seams.

4. Sew rectangles for skirt together in the same manner as for slip skirt, leaving 4" opening at top of back center seam. Gather top edge of skirt and pin to bottom edge of dress top; stitch. Hem open edges of back of dress and bottom of skirt.

5. Cut a 2" wide strip of fabric for the neckband long enough for the neck edge of the dress top plus two 1/4" end seams. Fold in half lengthwise, right sides together, and sew end seams. With right sides together sew neck band to neck edge of dress top. Fold under 1/4" along other side and slip-stitch to inside edge of dress top.

6. Add buttons or snaps to back opening. Add trim or pockets to dress as desired.

Pinafore.
1. Cut: 2 Pinafore Tops (on fold)
2 Pinafore Ruffles (on fold)
two 2" x 15" waistbands
one 10" x 44" rectangle for skirt (or two 10" x 22" rectangles sewn together)

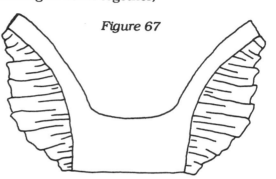

Figure 67

2. Fold Pinafore Ruffles in half lengthwise, wrong sides together. Gather raw edges. Pin each ruffle to right side of outer edge of Pinafore Top as shown. Place the second Pinafore Top on top, right side down. Stitch outer edge. Sew neck edge, being very careful not to catch the ruffle in the seam. Turn right side out.

3. Hem bottom and sides of pinafore skirt. Gather the top. Sew pinafore skirt, ribbons, and pinafore bib to waistband as shown.

Figure 68

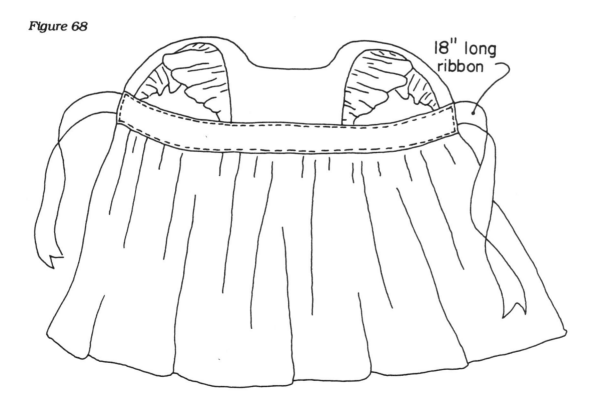

18" long ribbon

Shoes.
1. Cut: 2 Shoe Sides and 2 opposite Shoe Sides
   1 Shoe Flap and one opposite Shoe Flap
   2 Shoe Soles

Figure 69

2. With right sides together sew Shoe Flap to Shoe Side (a). Place the opposite Shoe Side on top, right side down; stitch toe and back of shoe (b). Sew on Shoe Sole. Turn right side out. If desired, glue a smaller cardboard shoe sole inside for added stiffness. Repeat for other shoe.

(a) 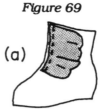 (b)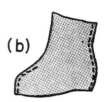

3. Cut small slits in Shoe Flaps for button holes. Put shoes on doll's feet and mark location for buttons. Take shoes off and sew on buttons.

Figure 70. Pattern pieces for Heirloom Doll.

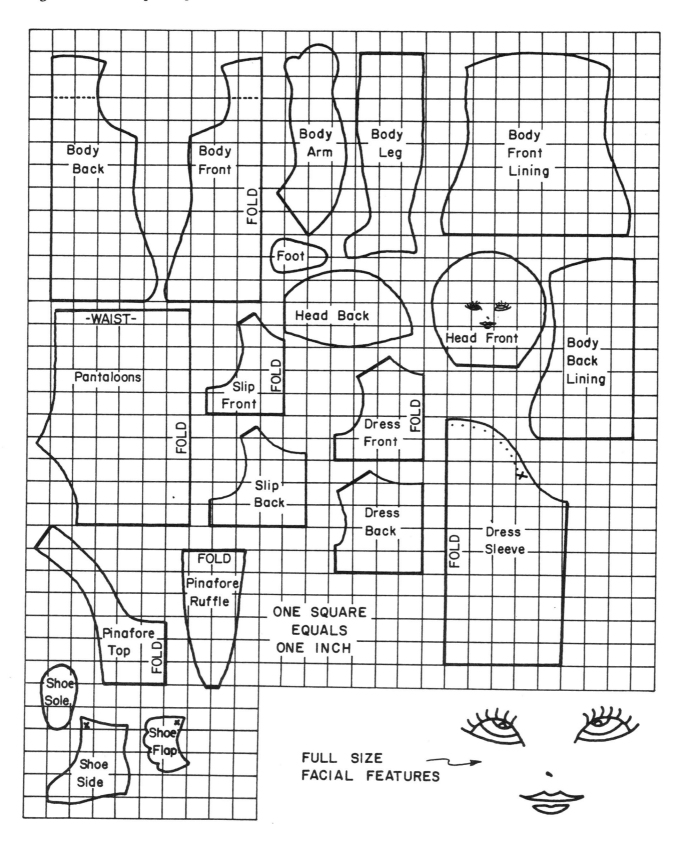

FAMILY QUILT

Creating a family quilt in which everyone has contributed a square can be a fun and profitable project. There are several ways to handle it. You could include a note in the reunion notices asking everyone to bring a completed square of a specific size to the reunion. During the gathering anyone who wants to can help piece the blocks together. The quilt top could then be raffled or auctioned off (requiring the lucky recipient to add batting and bottom lining and finish it or pay someone else to do this), or one person could arrange to have the cover finished into a quilt before the next reunion -- when it would be raffled or auctioned.

Another option is to have people make the squares during the reunion and a committee does the rest of the work before the next reunion. In this case you will need to have fabric squares and permanent fabric markers ready for use at the reunion. Encourage each person to decorate one square and sign his or her name to it.

Keep in mind that many people would much prefer an afghan-size lap quilt to a full-size bed quilt. A lap quilt should be approximately 50" to 60" wide and 65" to 82" long; be sure to use a warm, cuddly fabric such as flannel for the lining. These are great to use in the living room for extra warmth while watching TV or as a decorating accent. It's also nice to have one in the car when doing any traveling.

See page 129 for more notes on this subject.

FRAMED NEEDLEWORK

Photo 25: Courtesy of Stanton Rickey. Emma Rickey crocheted two special wall hangings
for her family reunion -- one to be raffled off and one to present to a family member
in recognition of family history research efforts.

A framed piece of beautiful needlework which has been designed and stitched by a family member makes a great raffle or auction item. It could be a "Bless this Family" sampler, or one or more of the following could be incorporated into the design: the family surname or coat of arms; names, birth dates, or marriage dates of ancestors; drawings of past or present family homes; family sayings, stories, or legends; a family chart or tree.

Browse through books in the needlecraft section at your public library for ideas. Use the enlargement or reduction features on a photocopying machine to enlarge or reduce designs to the desired size. One very helpful book is *Samplers: How to Create Your Own Designs* by Julia Milne (New York: Mallard Press, 1989). Also, the drawings in Fig. 71 - Fig. 75 may spark some ideas of your own. Feel free to incorporate any parts of these designs into your own creation.

Figure 71. Sample design with family surname.

Figure 72. A simple rendition of an ancestor's home is used in this design, along with the names of the couple and their children, and the names of the two families which were joined by this marriage.

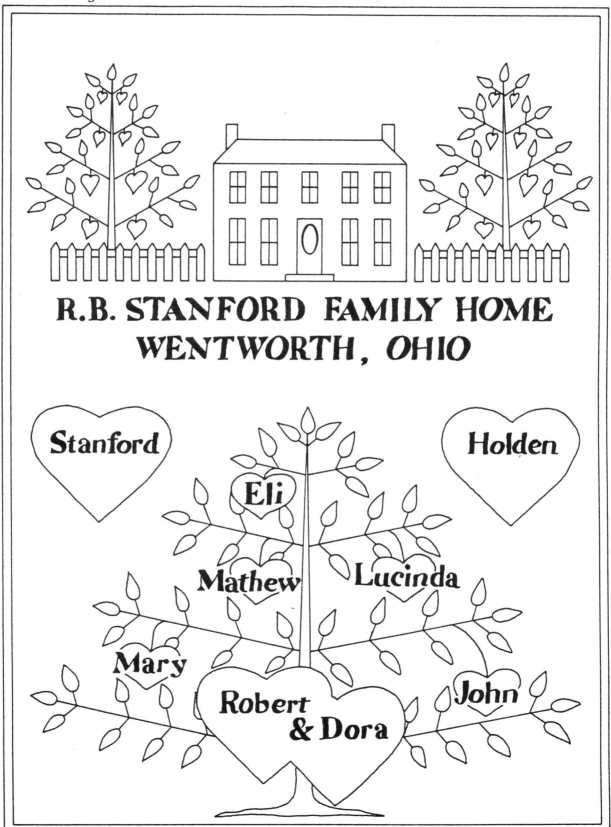

Figure 73. Sample design featuring the family surname and a sentiment about reunions.

Figure 74. Sample alphabet.

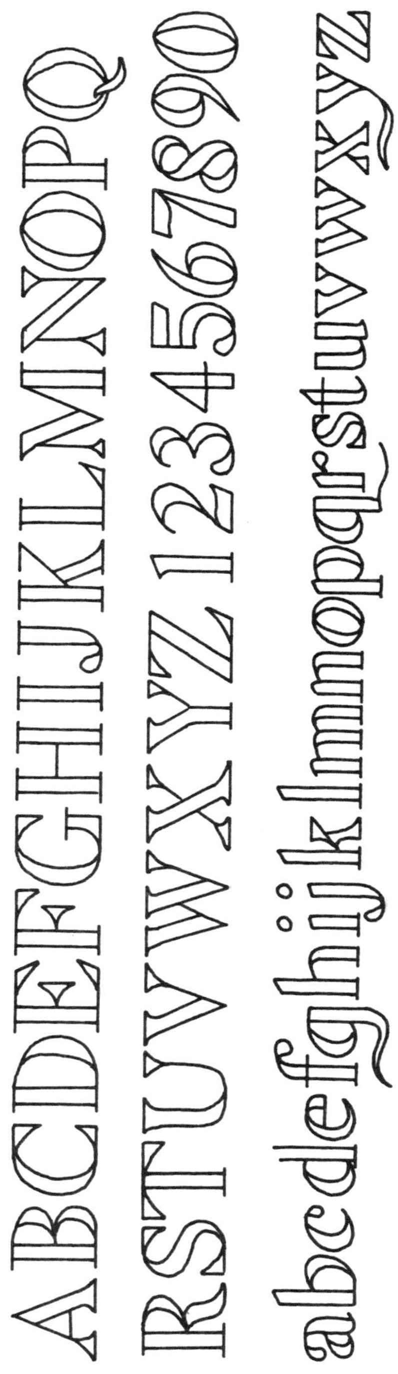

Figure 75. This humorous explanation of why there are so many Smiths in the world had been handed down from generation to generation. It becomes a charming wall hanging by adding a border and featuring the surname.

ITEMS TO GO ALONG WITH THE REUNION THEME

Suppose you decide that this year the reunion theme will be 'Christmas in July' (a really fun theme to carry out and very popular with the kids!). Spread the word for everyone to bring a homemade Santa Claus (or angel) for the family auction. If family members are located all across the United States, suggest that everyone might want to make use of items common in nature in the area where they live: shells, driftwood, natural local clay, cornshucks, etc. Think of all the things that a Santa could be made of: papier-maché, a piece of carved firewood with thin birch bark slit and curled at the ends for a beard, velvet pieced in crazy-quilt style, etc. The Santas could be Christmas tree ornaments, a cross-stitched wall hanging, or embroidered designs on a pair of pillowcases. An unusual cane could be made by carving and painting a Santa head on the larger end of an interesting stick found during a walk in the woods; imagine how a painted white beard flowing a third of the way down the stick would look. Even the children can contribute homemade Santas for the auction! The enjoyment of a project like this is threefold: the enjoyment of making your own unique Santa, the enjoyment at the reunion of seeing what everyone else created, and the enjoyment later at Christmas-time when you use the Santas you bought at the family auction and remember the feeling of love and kinship at the reunion.

If you are planning a patriotic theme for your reunion you might asked for red, white, and blue or patriotic items. Aunt Jane, who is known for her very fine stitches, might make a homemade flag -- sure to be a treasured keepsake of the highest bidder or the lucky winner of the raffle. Someone else might make an Uncle Sam doll or an eagle carved out of wood. Compile a special book of stories about ancestors who have served our country; include memories -- humorous, touching, or sad -- of living relatives about their experiences while in the U.S. Armed Services.

AUTOGRAPH TEDDY BEAR

Use any teddy bear pattern and cream-colored sailcloth to make an autograph teddy bear. Use a fabric marker to print the name and year of the reunion on the center front of the bear before sewing the pattern pieces together. Stuff the bear very firmly to make it easier to sign and tie a pretty bow around the neck.

Ask everyone present at the reunion to sign the teddy bear with colorful fabric markers or felt pens; explain that it will be auctioned or raffled off later for a good cause -- to help pay for future reunions! Note: this also makes a wonderful gift for the newest baby in the family; print "Welcome To The (surname) Family" on the front.

Depending on what your family surname is you might want to adapt this idea to match the surname. For instance, if your name is Brown your 'Brown Bear' could be made from brown sailcloth and signed with white fabric markers. If your surname is Lamb, use a stuffed lamb instead of a teddy bear.

BOOK OF OLD TIME CRAFTS, TOYS, AND GAMES

Ask the older generation about what they did for fun when they were young and make a book out of what you find out. Grandma may remember making hollyhock dolls and using bugle vine blooms for long fingernails when playing the part of the evil witch in Hansel and Gretel. Uncle John and Aunt Grace may recall spending hours with the neighborhood kids playing a game called Andyover. Record their memories of how the game was played and what it meant when someone yelled "Pigtail!". Maybe Grandpa knows how to make a special type of braided cord with an empty wooden thread spool and some finishing nails pounded into one end. Make a drawing and step-by-step instructions.

Ask around and you'll probably have more than enough stories, drawings, instructions, and photos for a very unique book on old-time fun, games, and crafts. There will probably be several family members who would like a copy of this book so publish several of them instead of just one. Each copy should be numbered as in "No. 3 of 15". Make copy No. 1 even more valuable by having the people included in the book sign the page about themselves.

UNFORGETTABLE PEOPLE IN THE _____ FAMILY

Ask each of the older people in the family to write about a relative -- perhaps the oldest relative they can remember or one who really stands out in childhood memories. Assemble the collection in book form and title it 'Unforgettable People in the _____ Family'.

One oldster might remember a little story about his Grandpa Elliott: "People used to always get mixed up on how many Ls and Ts there were in his name, so he finally made a jingle about it. He would tell them 'E-double L-I-O-double T, if that ain't right it oughta be!'. Somehow that jingle would always stick in people's minds and they would never have to ask him again how to spell Elliott."

There are usually relatives -- now dead -- who made a big impression on your older aunts and uncles when they were young. Often there is a single scene or act that remains vivid in their mind, such as a great uncle who had a bear rug in the middle of his living room and delighted in using it to scare the dickens out of little kids! Or the grandmother who used to sneak extra cookies to the grandchildren as they were leaving after a visit -- behind the backs of the parents who had said no to any more sweets.

Who are those unforgettable people in your family's past who implanted lifelong memories in the young minds of their descendants? Share them with your descendants.

BOOK OF MEMORIES

This is another book that you might want to make several copies of to sell for the family reunion fund. The memories included aren't necessarily from just the older generation in the family, although you should be sure to include theirs. Young children could be asked what their earliest memory about a grandparent is. You may be surprised at the answer. If you are asking the question of someone who is eight years old or younger, he will very likely not remember that memory when he is grown. Wouldn't this book be a great present for him or her years from now?

Things that were a part of everyday life for one generation are often very interesting and educational to future generations. For instance, do you know why a jar of water was kept beside hand water pumps and why a person was likely to catch the dickens if he or she forgot to refill the jar after pumping some water? If you are directing a team of horses, which way is 'gee' and which way is 'haw'? Do you have relatives who know the rules for planting by the signs (and what is their version of the rules)? Does someone remember the time Grandad Williamson bought a 'Sears catalog house'? What disasters have your relatives lived through or been told about?

Are there any favorite sayings in the family, such as Grampa Ralph's "What is to be will be, and what ain't just might happen!". What did ancestral homes which no longer exist look like? What is the story behind the brick that your two great uncles exchanged in church every Christmas? What miracles or mysterious things have happened to members of the family?

Ask people for details. Did great-great grampa speak softly or with a booming voice? When he lifted you up to his lap, could you feel any blisters on his hands or were they smooth? What did his favorite hat look like? Was he usually happy, sad, quiet, funny, busy, cautious? Who kept watch beside the bed the night he died?

If you plan to ask for written contributions for this book through the mail you will probably get the best results by explaining what you are doing in a short letter on one side of a sheet of paper. Remind the person that it is for a worthy cause (family reunions that everyone can afford to attend) and include a self addressed stamped envelope. Include a short list of possible topics, and suggest that they use the back side of the sheet to reply. Ask for a reply within two weeks so that they do not lay the letter aside and forget it.

Have patience. Some people really don't believe they could have anything to write which would be of interest to anyone else. Convince them that they are wrong.

Figure 76. Two people might want to work together on a page. For instance, a grandmother supplies the writing while her granddaughter supplies the drawing.

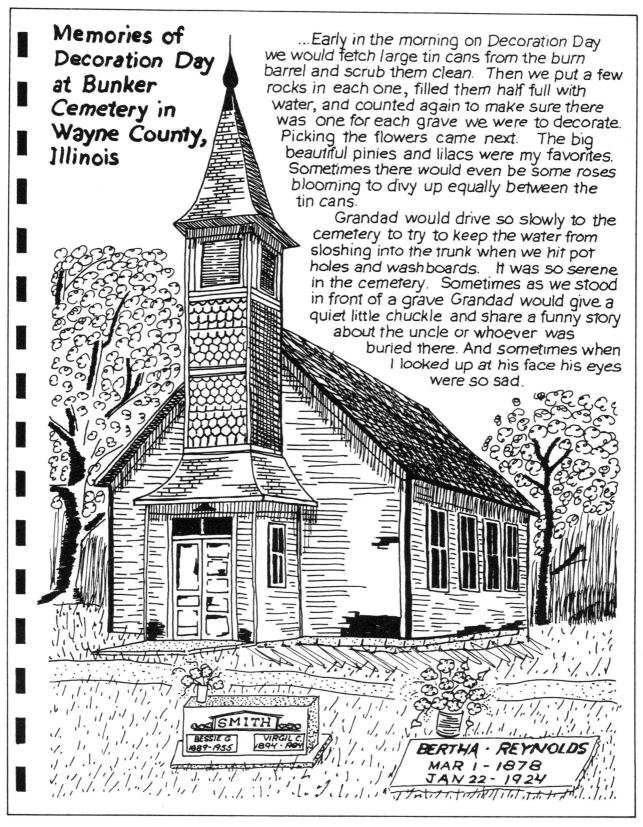

Memories of Decoration Day at Bunker Cemetery in Wayne County, Illinois

...Early in the morning on Decoration Day we would fetch large tin cans from the burn barrel and scrub them clean. Then we put a few rocks in each one, filled them half full with water, and counted again to make sure there was one for each grave we were to decorate. Picking the flowers came next. The big beautiful pinies and lilacs were my favorites. Sometimes there would even be some roses blooming to divy up equally between the tin cans.

Grandad would drive so slowly to the cemetery to try to keep the water from sloshing into the trunk when we hit pot holes and washboards. It was so serene in the cemetery. Sometimes as we stood in front of a grave Grandad would give a quiet little chuckle and share a funny story about the uncle or whoever was buried there. And sometimes when I looked up at his face his eyes were so sad.

SMITH

BESSIE G
1889-1955

VIRGIL C.
1894-1964

BERTHA · REYNOLDS
MAR 1 - 1878
JAN 22 - 1924

DID YOU KNOW...? TRIVIA BOOK ABOUT YOUR FAMILY

This would be a great project for the family historian and a teenager to work on together. The book they compile would contain interesting tidbits of information about the family that even those people who are not terribly interested in genealogy would like to read -- things that make you chuckle or say "Hmmm."

For instance, a grandfather in one family has his name (and birth date) on two headstones in two different graveyards which are several miles apart. Why?

A person who was tracing his family line came across a relative named Shadrack Meshack Abednego Rogers. The grandchildren fondly remembered calling him Shadrack Meshack and Under-the-bed-we-go.

A old deed to some family land showed that in 1859 Benjamin F. Cunningham and Sarah M. Cunningham sold land to Bradford Cooper on one condition: "...no spirituous liquor be sold there nor hogs raised running at large." Why?

The book of tidbits could also include items such as unusual photos (three older men all standing on their heads), advertisements from old newspapers about businesses that belonged to relatives, a marriage license where the bride obviously lied about her age, etc.

Figure 77. Advertisement of a great grandfather's business in a 1954 telephone book.

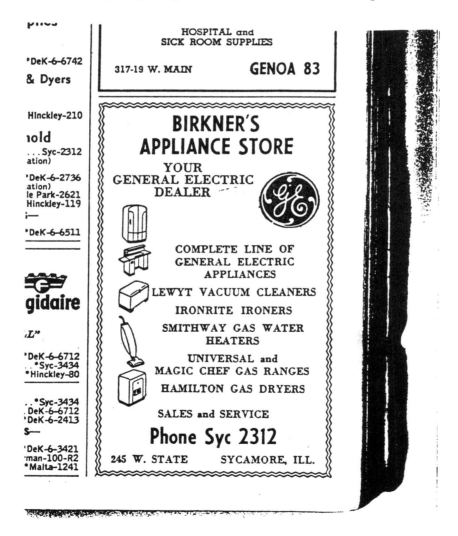

COOKBOOK

Many families have put together a collection of favorite family recipes. These cookbooks become treasured keepsakes and also make wonderful gifts for friends. There are as many ways to put together a cookbook as there are types of families; reading about what has worked for others might help you decide on the best method for your family.

When Mary Katherine Townsend of Texas volunteered to organize the creation of a family cookbook for her family she first mailed double (folded) recipe cards -- stamped and addressed -- to relatives on the reunion list and friends who always attend Kelly reunions:

"To aunts and uncles who had several children I mailed several cards and asked them to get them to their children," she says. "Also, there was a contest for the first to be received -- a free book. The last to be received had to wear a cow's tail at the reunion; this helped get recipes in early!"

Figure 78. You may want to photocopy some recipes to preserve the handwriting as well as the recipe. Notice that this meatloaf recipe specifies 40 cents worth of hamburger. Does that give you an idea of how long ago it was written!

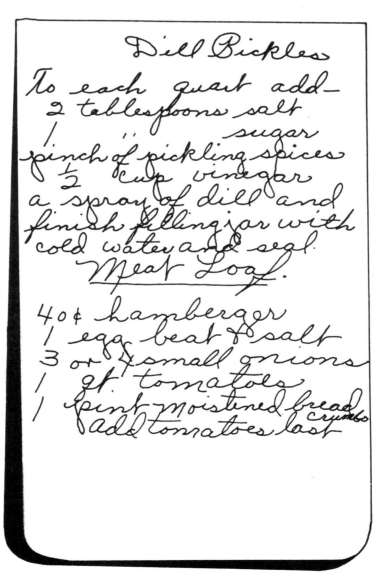

Selected relatives in key cities served on telephone committees which helped prod people into sending in recipes. "When I had received about 150 recipes I counted each category," says Mary Katherine. "I put the word out what we needed more of -- soups, appetizers, etc. I asked people who made these things especially well to send more recipes." The Kelly family holds a cooking contest during each reunion, and past contest-winning recipes were indicated in the cookbook with a little apron and the year drawn above the recipe.

Don't limit yourself to just food recipes when considering what types of recipes to include. Ruth Brown of Indiana writes: "One cousin had a recipe for a healing salve that our great-great-grandfather had perfected. It was put in the front of the Boehm Family cookbook. Several other original recipes of his were also found and included." Old, original recipes are always popular.

You might want to include other special touches in your cookbook, as did the family of Brenda Gotensky of Michigan. "My one aunt in Pennsylvania made up a poem for our reunion," says Brenda, "and it's published in our cookbook". On the cover is a drawing of the grandparents' home.

The time required for this project varies but the average time is probably one year -- agreeing to do the project at one reunion and having the finished books ready to sell at the following reunion. Allow yourself time to deal with procrastinators and to proofread the book.

Roberta Mingyar of West Virginia recalls that the committee for the Himes-Shaffer Family Reunion Cookbook collected recipes for over two years: "Many would promise to give us recipes but it took repeated reminders before they would sit down and write their favorite recipes for us. Some had made dishes, etc. for years but had never taken time to write them down on paper." Yet another family mailed the original letters asking for recipes in March and had finished cookbooks in September.

Some people prefer to handle the entire cookbook project by themselves; others want help. The McEwen Dawson Family Reunion cookbook project was handled by a committee of eight people. In another family two people were in charge -- each taking care of one major branch of the family -- and these two appointed other people to help.

Estimating the number of cookbooks to publish can be a bit tricky. Generally the larger the number of books the less expensive each book so you want to publish as many as you can use. Publishing too many, however, can eat up the profits. Phyllis Rhodes of New Mexico reports that her family (which averages about seventy-five people at the Lemaster/Patterson Reunions) ordered 300 books and sold out within three months. When Beverly Bauda helped to put together a collection of her 89-year-old Italian grandmother's favorite recipes she ordered 110 cookbooks. These were quickly sold out. Another order was placed with the cookbook publishing company. And another. And another. The cookbook is still going strong.

Another decision to be made at the start of the project is whether to take orders and money in advance. If not, someone will have to come up with money to pay for the printing until the cookbooks are sold. Martha Grubbs of Kentucky reports that the members of her family's cookbook committee donated the amount needed to put down a deposit for the cookbooks. Roberta Mingyar of West Virginia suggests: "If you do not have enough money to send the advance payment a member of the family who has confidence and trust in the project may advance the money and be willing to wait until enough cookbooks are sold to repay the amount that was advanced. This is what we did. We had no problems."

One experienced family cookbook organizer has the following suggestions for anyone considering putting together a similar project: First, make the initial book unique by having a front sheet (inside the front cover) describing the book as original. Second, number the original copies, i.e. 1/200, 2/200, 3/200 meaning No. 1 of 200, No. 2 of 200, and so on. Third, have the people who put together the cookbook either sign or initial the originals. Fourth, generate interest in the originals by pointing out that it will be a limited edition -- to be numbered and signed or initialed. Fifth, don't underestimate the potential for these books to become treasured heirlooms.

You will need to decide at the beginning of the project how and by whom the book will be printed. If you want to use a commercial publisher you will probably find that companies who specialize in printing cookbooks (for fundraising for churches, organizations) can do the job more inexpensively than your local print shops. Find out what they have to offer, what they provide, and in what form they want the recipes before you begin collecting them. Many companies will supply you with recipe collection forms at no extra charge. Most publishers require four to five months from the time you send them the recipes to the time they send you the finished, bound cookbooks.

Here is a list of cookbook publishing companies that you might want to check out:

1. Fundcraft
   410 Highway 72 W
   P.O. Box 340
   Collierville, TN 38017
       (901) 853-7070
       (800) 351-7822

2. Cookbook Publishers, Inc.
2101 Kansas City Road
   P.O. Box 1260
   Olathe, KS 66061-1260
   (913) 764-5900
   (800) 227-7282

3. The Recipe Express
   1008 Manchester Lane
   Charlotte, NC 28227
       (704) 568-2949

4. Circulation Service, Inc.
   P.O. Box 7306
   Indian Creek Station
       Leawood, KS 66207
       (913) 491-6300

5. Morris Press
3212 E. Hwy 30
P.O. Box 1681
Kearney, NE 68848
    (308) 236-7888
    (800) 445-6621

6. G & R Publishing Co.
   507 Industrial Street
   Waverly, Iowa 50677
       (800) 383-1679
       FAX: 319-352-5338

Write or call for their information literature and samples. Keep these questions in mind when deciding which one to use:
1. What is included in the basic cost?
2. What is the minimum order size accepted?
3. What are the payment terms?
4. In what form do they want the recipes submitted?
5. How long will it take from the time you send them the recipes until they ship you the finished cookbooks?
6. What kinds of covers are offered: generic, imprinted with the family name, custom designed? Are the covers plastic or laminated for extra durability?
7. What kind of binding do they use: 3 ring binder, spiral wire binding, plastic comb binding?
8. How large is the print? This could be very important to older members of the family.
9. How many categories do they divide the recipes into?
10. Will there be an index?
11. Can you include a photo or a few pages about your family at the front of the book?
12. Can an order form be included at the back of the book for people who would like to buy additional copies? This can result in a lot of additional sales; be sure to state who the check or money order should be made out to, the address to mail the order to, the price of cookbook, and mailing charge.

Some people prefer to type and print the books themselves. Freida Price of Illinois used her own copier and limited the cookbook for her family to twenty-five sheets printed on both sides. She used clear plastic report covers with colored spines to bind the pages. "These will hold twenty-five sheets exactly and not one sheet more," she advises.

In case you decide to organize and print the cookbook yourself one step-by-step method is described below. The advantage of this particular method is that it can be done in steps; when one step is completed the project can be set aside until you have another block of time available for working on it.

STEP 1. Ask family members for their favorite recipes. Suggest how many you would like to receive from each person. Ask them to type or print plainly.

STEP 2. Type the recipes -- one recipe on one 8 1/2" x 11" sheet. (Yes, I realize this will be wasting the bottoms of a lot of sheets, but it saves time in the long run and makes the project more manageable by being able to do it a part at a time). Keep the margins uniform. Proofread each recipe.

STEP 3. Separate the recipe sheets into categories (meats, vegetables, etc.). The number and kinds of categories you use will depend on what kinds of recipes are submitted. For instance, while one family might have one DESSERTS category, another family might have so many in this category that they decide to divide it into four separate categories: PIES AND COBBLERS, COOKIES AND BARS, CAKES AND FROSTINGS, and MISCELLANEOUS DESSERTS.

STEP 4. Now comes the cutting and pasting part. Take one category of recipes. Cut a recipe from one sheet (cut horizontally only -- from one side to the other) and paste it onto another sheet using rubber cement. Only after the recipes have been typed can you tell how much space they take and how many will fit on one sheet (i.e. one long and two mediums, or two longs). Hint: use the sheets with the longest recipes as the base sheets and shuffle around the other recipes until they fit the remaining spaces. Keep top and bottom margins uniform on the finished sheets.

STEP 5. Once you have finished cutting and pasting each category you will know how many pages you have and can make a mock-up of the finished book. Use half sheets of typing paper or scrap paper to do this. Write the titles of the recipes on the mock-up pages; remember that two of your cut-and-paste sheets will equal one double-sided finished page.

You will probably want the first page of each category to be on a righthand page to make it easier to find when flipping through the book. If you end up with a blank page for the last page of the preceding category you can either find additional recipes to fill the page or use a filler (Fig. 80 and Fig. 81). A few pages of humor scattered here and there can liven up the book. You could also include a photo of a family feast or a written recollection about something that happened in the kitchen or during the preparation of a family reunion meal.

Add mock-ups of any other pages you want to include: a title page, dedication, page thanking those who submitted recipes or helped to pay for the book, pages telling something of the history of the family, etc. After deciding what these pages should include on the mock-up, go ahead and make the actual pages.

One note about any photographs that you might want to use: your photographs will reproduce much better if you first have a 'half-tone' made of them. Take the photograph to a print shop (shop around for prices) and ask them to make a half-tone. If you plan to use more than one photo you can save money by taping as many as will fit on an 8 1/2" x 11" piece of plain paper. You will be charged for that size anyhow -- whether it is one photo in the center or covered with photos -- so you might as well get your money's worth. The print shop can make black-and-white half-tones from color or black-and-white photos. If possible try to keep photos of about the same darkness on the same sheet, otherwise the half-tone process may end up getting one photo too dark in an effort to get another one dark enough.

STEP 6. Put all of the 8 1/2" x 11" sheets together in order with each two pages that make up a single double-sided sheet placed back to back. Number all the sheets. Now is the time to add any clip art or simple drawings wherever there is extra space, such as in between two recipes that didn't quite use the whole page but there wasn't room for another recipe. Small cooking type drawings (a pie, a pot with steam rising, etc.) will make a page more visually attractive.

STEP 7. If you don't have your own copier go to one print shop for a price estimate. Tell them what you are doing and how many copies you need. Look at what they have available for colors, weights for covers, etc. Write down the specifics of what you want and ask them to call you with a quote on how much they will charge for the job, including binding if you will need that service. Once you have written down the specifics for the job you can call two or three other print shops for quotes and compare prices.

You might ask if anyone in the family can borrow a plastic comb binding machine from their workplace. If so you can buy the plastic comb binders from an office supply store and make a party one night or weekend out of assembling and binding all the copies. This will reduce your binding costs considerably.

Figure 79. Be sure to include the name of ther person who supplied the recipe. Highlight the recipe title in some way. Don't forget to use white correction fluid to conceal any unwanted edge lines resulting from your cut-and-paste job.

Linda Jeorgason's

OLD FASHIONED APPLE BUTTER

Mash, quarter, and core: 8 lbs tart apples (about 20).
Combine with: 8 cups apple cider in large baking pan. Cover.
Cook on top of range 20 minutes or until apples are very
soft. Strain to remove skins. Return pulp to pan.
Stir in: 4 cups sugar
        2 tsp cinnamon
        1/2 tsp nutmeg
        1/4 tsp allspice
        1/8 tsp ground cloves
Simmer uncovered, stirring often, 2 hours or until thick.
Slide baking pan into 350° oven. Bake, stirring
occasionally, 2 hours or until richly brown and very thick.
Pour into sterilized jars.

John Devore's

RHUBARB JAM

6 cups rhubarb, sliced small
4 1/2 cups sugar

Boil 20 minutes; start over a low slow heat.
Remove from heat and add 1 pkg red jello.
Stir until dissolved. Pour in glasses and seal (refrigerate).

Nancy Devore's

RHUBARB APRICOT JAM

In a heavy saucepan cook 8 oz moist dried apricots(quartered)
in water to cover. Drain, reserving 2 cups liquid.
Add
        1 tlb grated orange peel
        1 large orange, peeled & sectioned & membrane removed
        1 lb. rhubarb, cut in 1/2 to 3/4" pieces
        3 cups sugar
Heat to simmering. Stir. Cook over low heat, stirring often
about 40 minutes til mixture is of thick jam. Watch
carefully. Mixture burns easily. Makes about 3 cups.

133

Figure 80. Add a little humor. Start with a photo and improvise. The idea for this page began with a snapshot of a grandmother which had been taken right after someone had placed a white sack on her head for a chef's hat. The photo was cut off at mid-chest, removing all background, and a few lines were added to make it look like she's sitting at a table.

Figure 81. Ask around and see if anyone has any farce recipes or menus.

GERRY'S SPECIAL MENU

MONDAY
Breakfast: weak tea
Lunch: 1 bouillon cube in 1 cup diluted water
Dinner: 1 pigeon thigh, 3 oz prune juice (gargle only)

TUESDAY
Breakfast: scraped crumbs from burnt toast
Lunch: 1 donut hole without sugar
Dinner: mosquito legs sauteed in vinegar

WEDNESDAY
Breakfast: shredded egg shell skin
Lunch: 1/2 doz poppy seeds
Dinner: 3 grains cornmeal - broiled

THURSDAY
Breakfast: boiled out stains of old tablecloth
Lunch: belly button of a navel orange
Dinner: 3 Idaho potato eyes, diced & steamed

FRIDAY
Breakfast: 4 chopped banana seeds
Lunch: broiled butterfly liver
Dinner: Visions of Sugar Plums, 4 min. only

SATURDAY
Breakfast: 2 lobster antennas
Lunch: one barbequed tail joint of sea horse
Dinner: rotisserie broiled guppy fillet

SUNDAY
Breakfast: pickled hummingbird tongue
Lunch: prime rib of tadpole
Dinner: tossed paprika and clover leaf salad

ENJOY!

Figure 82. A page of thank yous is always appreciated.

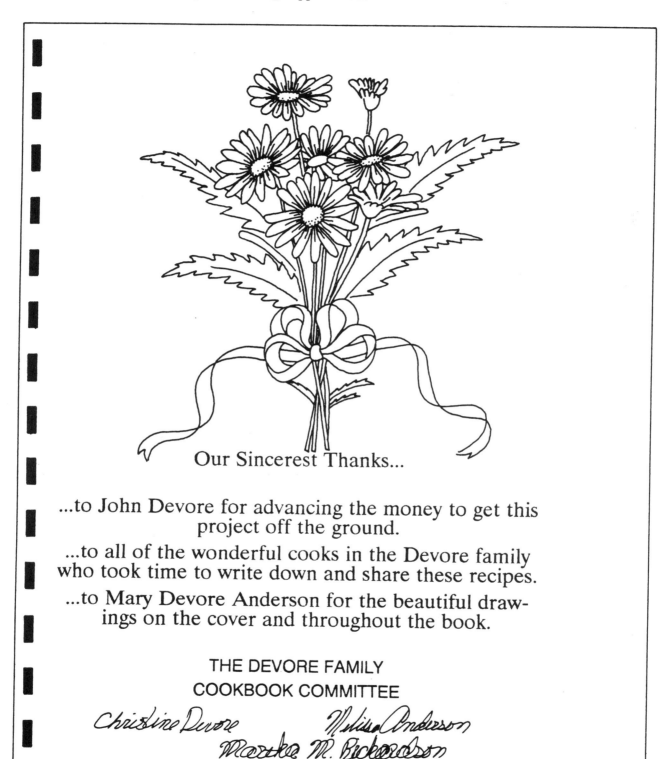

Our Sincerest Thanks...

...to John Devore for advancing the money to get this project off the ground.

...to all of the wonderful cooks in the Devore family who took time to write down and share these recipes.

...to Mary Devore Anderson for the beautiful drawings on the cover and throughout the book.

THE DEVORE FAMILY
COOKBOOK COMMITTEE

Christine Devore   Melissa Anderson
Martha M. Richardson

Figure 83. Don't feel that you must fill every bit of space on a page; white space can be very effective. Carefully cutting away all the background in a photo often makes a better illustration.

**Dedicated to
Grampa
Samuel Hindenburg.**

**You nourished
our souls
with heirloom love
and
keepsake memories.**

Special Family Projects

Reunions give relatives a chance to visit with each other, catch up on what's happening in each other's lives, and enjoy that feeling of belonging in a special group of people. Having a special project to work on together enhances that feeling of kinship and unity. It could be a year-round project, such as publishing a family newsletter, or a one-time event such as a one-day clean-up of a neglected family cemetery. The purpose of the project could be to help keep family members in touch between reunions, to raise money for the next reunion, to create a keepsake such as a family cookbook, or to preserve some part of your heritage.

Here are some ideas for special family projects:

BUDGET OR ROUND-ROBIN LETTER

The Elliott Family has for years circulated what they call a budget letter among family members in several states who wish to participate. This type of letter (also called a round-robin letter) is started by a member in one family writing a letter about what is going on in his or her family -- day to day happenings, special accomplishments, etc. He sends the letter to another family that wants to participate. The second family reads the first letter, adds their own letter, and sends it on to a third family. This continues until the last person who wants to participate receives the letter. That family reads the rest of the letters, adds their own, and sends it back to the first person on the list. In the succeeding rounds, each family reads all the letters and replaces their old letter with a new one. (By the way, since these letters highlight what is going on in your life, why not save all of your old letters for fascinating reading for your descendants someday!)

The length of time required for the letter to make a complete round depends on how many stops it makes, how far apart the stops are, and how long each person takes to read the letters and add their own. It's a great way for cousins to find out what each other's lives are like and requires only one letter to the group -- as opposed to a separate letter to each family. The advantage of this method over a newsletter is that no one has to volunteer to be editor and publisher, and it is somehow 'friendlier' than most newsletters. The only cost to each person is a new envelope and three stamps or however much postage is required to send it on its way. One possible hang-up is that some people are procrastinators -- they receive the family letter, enjoy reading about what everyone else is doing, and mean to write a new letter and get it back in the mail but they keep procrastinating until the phone lines are busy with everyone trying to figure out who put the budget letter on top of their refrigerator and forgot it.

Be sure everyone is invited to participate, and no one is made to feel guilty if they decide to drop out of the circle temporarily or permanently because they are just too busy. Your next reunion would be a great time to organize this project. Write down all the addresses of those who want to be included, decide the best path for the circle to follow, and get it going.

The Elliott family keeps a typed list of all participants in the budget letter itself. It includes the name of the person in the family who usually writes the letter, the names of his or her children and spouse, address, and telephone number. This helps everyone keep track of who belongs to whom and provides a place for address corrections.

FAMILY NEWSLETTER OR NEWSPAPER

Wanda Copeland of Indiana expresses very well why the little newspaper her niece edits and publishes quarterly for the family is so important and worthwhile: "When families are so scattered nowadays this little paper is such a blessing. This family communique, as well as our yearly reunions, truly serves to keep our family in close touch with one another. Besides, it is a tangible legacy we are leaving for those who follow us. It leaves something of our personalities, our doings, and ourselves so that they know from where and whom they came."

Members of her family have a deadline for sending letters, family information, wedding notices, obituaries, congratulations, newspaper clippings, and "anything special or not so special that makes family history" to the niece, who types it up, makes copies, and mails out *Hicks Happenings* to each family member who subscribes ($5.00 per year). One special feature in the newspaper is an article written by an adult in the family (starting with the oldest and continuing down) about their life from birth to the present. If the person is married it is about both the husband and wife.

"A list of suggestions for their story telling is sent to each so they won't leave out anything," says Wanda. "There have been some great stories."

Wanda edits and publishes another family newsletter for the other side of the family, *Copeland Pathways: A Family Communique of Adventures.* The second heading on the front page explains the purpose of the newsletter succinctly: "Individually we travel far and wide down life's pathways; we touch the thorns, we climb to the peaks. Here, we keep in touch as one big family, sharing with each other our trek; thus we shorten the distance between us."

Figure 84. Courtesy of Wanda Copeland. List of ideas for the person writing a feature article for one family newsletter.

The following is a guideline to help you write the FEATURE ARTICLE for the next issue of "Copeland Pathways".

The deadline date is _____.

Use your full name.

Write your story (history) in chronological order.

Write your story as if someone who doesn't know you or anything about you is going to read it.

Name locations and dates - be as precise as you can be. If you cannot then generalize, such as "When I was around 10...", or "When we lived near such and such...".

Tell as much as possible about each thing you are writing about and in plain direct sentences. Story form.

Start with who you are and about your birth--when, where, and anything interesting or unique; your parents and your siblings; anyone that might have lived in your home and was a part of your life.

Places you lived as a child.

What it was like when you were growing up: home life, entertainment, chores, early jobs, special toys, pets, special vacations, happenings/things that were important to you as a child, happy/sad and good/bad times.

School history: where, when, special teachers, interesting happenings, honors, sports, etc. Any clubs, hobbies, etc. (such as 4-H). Things you liked to do/did when growing up. Tough/good times.

Travel.

Special happenings.

First car, etc.

On into adulthood: higher education, employment/retirement, special honors, clubs, sports, hobbies, etc. If married, how did you meet, your courtship, wedding, honeymoon, children--many special stories here.

Where you've lived as an adult.

Church affiliations, etc.

KEEP IN MIND - DATES, PLACES, NAMES, SPECIAL HAPPENINGS, FUNNY, SAD, IMPORTANT, INTERESTING, TOUGH TIMES... - THE THINGS THAT HAVE MADE YOU YOU TO THIS DATE.

TELL "YOUR" STORY. IF YOU ARE MARRIED YOUR MATE SEES THE SAME HAPPENING/ EXPERIENCE/STORY FROM A DIFFERENT ANGLE. TELL IT AS YOU EACH SEE IT.

PLEASE END YOUR ARTICLE WITH SOME GOOD WORDS OR ADVICE TO OUR YOUNG PEOPLE.

Make your family newsletter friendly, enthusiastic, and informative. If you have no experience in doing this kind of thing go to the public library and check out a couple of books on publishing a newsletter. You may not want to do anything as formal as what most of them give suggestions for but it's still a good place to start getting ideas. If yours is a fairly large family association you may want to appoint a publications committee to oversee the production of a newsletter. The committee chooses an editor, decides how much to charge each subscriber for the newsletter, etc.

The *Robinett Family Newsletter and Journal* began in 1982 as two typewritten pages but now averages thirty-six pages, commercially copied and distributed to 600 members. It is published quarterly and includes Robinett Family Association business news, personal notes, obituaries, feature stories, genealogy, and photos. The editor, Jessie Robinette of Tennessee, types all written materials on a computer (leaving space for photos) and sends the pages and original photos to a relative in Florida. This person takes them to a nearby printing company which makes half-tones from the photos (half-tones print better than photos), affixes them in the proper places, and turns out finished journals in about one week (for about $1.65 per copy). The copies are then labeled and mailed to Robinett Family Association members.

Figure 85. Courtesy of Bert Frye. The front cover of this family newsletter features a sketch of an ancestor's stone house.

Here are items you might want to include in your family newsletter:
1. information about the next family reunion
2. a summary about the last reunion
3. family members in the news
4. treasurer's report
5. membership report
6. obituaries
7. a queries section for people in or out of your family association who need help with ancestor hunting
8. letter from the reunion president
9. news about family members currently serving in the U.S. military
10. address changes for family members
11. "Did You Know...?" section for interesting tidbits of information about your family -- past or present
12. puzzle or quiz pertaining to the family's history
13. open letters from family members
14. closing date for submitting articles for the next issue

REUNION SCRAPBOOK

Some families keep a record of each gathering in a reunion scrapbook. Roberta Mingyar of West Virginia reports that the Himes-Shaffer Family Reunion maintains a scrapbook of all news items, funeral notices, birth announcements, etc. Anyone can submit items for it to the family historian, who is in charge of updating the book and displaying it during reunions.

Sonia Cesarino of Pennsylvania says, "Our reunion has an 18" x 23" size reunion book. The first page has a picture and tells how the 'official' Bock Reunion was started. The reunion book also has family pages where we keep the genealogy and family pictures. Another feature is pictures of our servicemen. Finally, most of the book is taken up by pages of each individual reunion. Each year has a sign in sheet where everyone attending puts their name and address. There are also brief recollections of what happened at that reunion. We also have pictures of reunions, which is what takes up the most space. One of the most popular things at the reunion is looking through the reunion book and reminiscing. A lot of people enjoy seeing how the children grew from year to year, so we try to get lots of pictures of all the activities."

Below are listed some companies that offer archival scrapbooks and photo albums:

Light Impressions
    P.O. Box 940
    439 Monroe Avenue
    Rochester, NY 14607-0940
        (800) 828-6216 to order
        (800) 828-9859 for customer service
        FAX (716) 442-7318

Kusek Genealogical Services
    P.O. Box 32060
    Shawnee Msn., KS 66212-2060
        (913) 383-2458

Creative Memories
    2815 Clearwater Road
    P.O. Box 1839
    St. Cloud, MN 56301-1839
        (612) 251-3822, (800) 468-9335
        FAX (612) 251-6997
(They hold in-home workshops on creative photo preservation and are available to speak to organizations. Ask for the consultant in your area.)

RECORD OF FAMILY KEEPSAKES

This record could be contained in one section of the reunion scrapbook, or it could be a separate book.

Ask everyone to think about what family heirlooms and sentimental keepsakes they have in their possession, and request that they bring a photo of each item to the next reunion. (Bringing the actual article for display would be great, but this isn't always possible or practical.) These could be quilts, furniture, tools, clothing, bibles, letters, etc.

During the reunion make a written record to go with each photograph; include a description, where it originally came from, who owns it now, approximate age of the item, and what the significance of the item is to the family. One reason to do this at a group gathering such as a reunion is that other people in the family might be able to add information about the background of the item which can be included in the record (and would no doubt be of great interest to the person now in possession of it). For instance, one person might be in possession of an old Victrola cylinder record playing machine which once belonged to his father. Another person might remember the father saying that he had bought the Victrola for fifty cents at an auction for his mother, with money earned by picking blackberries for townspeople. An aunt might remember winter evenings long ago when the family would listen to the Victrola, and that the Uncle Josh records were the father's favorites. Including all these details makes the record much more interesting than recording only what the person in possession of it knows.

While everyone is taking stock of what items of historical significance they possess you might want to investigate how to properly preserve them for future generations -- particularly old documents. There are several businesses which sell this kind of supplies and services, such as:

The Preservation Emporium
 mail: P.O. Box 226309
 Dallas, TX 75222-6309
 store location: 2600 Stemmons Frwy, Suite 131
 Dallas, TX 75207
 (800) 442-2038 (orders only)
 (214) 630-1197 (questions)
 FAX (214) 630-7805

Ask for their catalog. They sell document cleaning materials, acid-free paper supplies, archival albums, document preservation storage kits, conservation 'how-to' books, etc. They also offer bookbinding and restoration services.

The Maryland State Archives offers a Paper Preservation Kit to help organize and preserve important family papers. For more information and prices contact the Maryland State Archives, 350 Rowe Boulevard, Annapolis, MD 21401, phone (301) 974-3914.

FAMILY WRITING CONTEST

Consider holding a contest for articles written about people or events in your family's history. After the John and Elizabeth Curtis/Curtiss Society published the Curtiss-Curtis Genealogy in 1953, the leaders of the Society thought that it might be interesting to have personal knowledge about some of those names:

"For the 1954 annual reunion they sponsored a story writing contest for the children of Society members," says Barbara Curtis Weaver of New York. "We were to select a family member that we knew or knew about that was listed in the genealogy. My parents encouraged me to write a story."

Barbara's story was titled "The Mighty Ephraim" and was about her great-grandfather; she won first place in the senior division. The first and second place winners in each division read their stories at the reunion and were presented with a trophy.

BOOK OF MEMORIALS

Mrs. Gene Odom of Georgia reports that the Ansley Family Association maintains a large, beautifully made book called a *Book of Memorials*. For $25.00 anyone in the family can dedicate a page to an ancestor and decide what he or she would like printed on the page (the person's name and lineage). The book already contains a great many entries, and is expandable so that more pages can be added as needed.

BOOK OF FAMILY HISTORY

Even if your family has not completed research on their heritage (if there is such a thing as 'completing' this kind of work) you might want to consider putting together what is known and printing copies for everyone. This type of book could also include a family directory for current addresses and telephone numbers of living family members, including ages, professions, anniversaries, and names of children.

If you are just getting interested in uncovering your family's history an excellent book to show you how to get started is *Unpuzzling Your Past: A Basic Guide to Genealogy*, by Emily Anne Croom (White Hall, Virginia: Betterway Publications, 1989). It is written in a very easy to read style.

Your family may also wish to add their collected genealogical data to the files of the Church of Jesus Christ of Latter-day Saints' Family History Library, the world's largest collection of genealogical information. The library welcomes gifts of genealogical information so that it can be shared with other researchers. There are more than 1,600 Family History Library branches in 57 countries; they are open to everyone, regardless of religious affiliations. If you would like more information about how to contribute your family data to their files contact the Family History Department, 50 East North Temple Street, Salt Lake City, Utah 84150, tel. (801) 240-2584.

If you are looking for a specialized album to record family data in, Reinecke Enterprizes offers a very nice looking Family Genealogy and History Album. If you would like more information about it send a self-addressed stamped envelope to Reinecke Enterprizes, Dept. R, P.O. Box 2406, Starkville, MS 39759 or call (800) 733-6770.

FAMILY COOKBOOK

Photo 26: Courtesy of Beverly Bauda. Beverly Bauda (right) spearheaded a labor of love--putting together a collection of favorite home-style Italian recipes of her grandmother, Josephine Quagliana (left).

Family reunions and good food go hand-in-hand and many families decide to collect all those wonderful recipes for a family reunion cookbook. This can be a fun project to start at one reunion and complete at the next. Everyone will look forward to receiving their own copy of this special family keepsake.

For more information on putting together a cookbook see pages 113-116. This can also be a great way to raise money to finance family reunions.

FAMILY QUILT

There's something about the words 'family quilt' that just sound warm and friendly.

"In the past at reunions we have done a quilt and cookbooks," says Freida Price of Illinois. "Both are fun and provide a carry-over and sense of anticipation for the next year."

She describes the process that was used the year she was in charge of putting together a family quilt for her family reunion:

"For the quilts, 16" muslin squares and Tri-chem or liquid embroidery paints are taken to the reunion. Each family who wants to buys a square for $2.50 and paints it in any way they like. The quality of the art is not important. Generally we use stick men figures. Sometimes there are apple trees with kids' names on each apple. Sometimes a family hobby is used such as a tent for camping with a person's name on sticks of firewood by the campfire. One family of four just traced their own hands. One man drives the church bus so we drew a bus and put enough heads in the windows for his family.

"Then a person in charge (me) takes the squares, sets them together with some donated cotton material and takes it to a lady in Litchfield, Illinois who furnishes the batting and quilts the whole thing by machine for $25.00. I had enough blocks to put blocks on both sides. When it was done I bound it and everyone who had their name on a block, no matter who put it there (grandma, aunt, etc.) got their name in the drawing and the drawing was held at high noon while everyone was seated and in one place. We did not have to sell chances because the $2.50 had paid the expenses and that's all I was interested in."

For additional comments on making a quilt see page 103.

MEMORY BOOK FOR AN ANNIVERSARY CELEBRATION/REUNION

Sometimes a family reunion is organized to help a couple celebrate a special anniversary, such as a 50th wedding anniversary. Why not plan ahead and make a truly special gift for them -- a memory book!

When sending out notices about the upcoming gathering in their honor, include a self-addressed stamped envelope and a piece of folded note paper with the following printed on one side:

> *We request your help in compiling a book that recalls memories about (name of couple) first fifty years of marriage. On the inside of this sheet we ask that you write some memories and experiences that you have shared with them and return it to us by (date). We believe that the loving memories they have shared with you, their friends and relatives, would be the most treasured gift they could receive; therefore we request that no other gift be sent.*
>
> *We look forward to hearing from you. Please help us keep this as a surprise for them on their special day of celebration.*

Display all of the letters received in a scrapbook and add other things pertinent to their married life: a copy of the marriage license, wedding photograph, photos of their first home, etc. Don't forget to give small children a chance to add their own letter to this collection, even if you have to do the writing while they dictate. Record their answers to questions such as "Why do you think Grampa loves Grandma so much? What makes Grandpa and Grandma so special to our family?" Out of the mouths of babes can come the most delightful answers! Also, have them make a crayon portrait of the couple.

FAMILY CEMETERY PROJECTS

There are a lot of cemeteries -- especially small ones -- in need of some tender loving care, and a lot of families who would benefit from working on a project together. Seems like a perfect match! Are some of your relatives buried in a cemetery which has been neglected? Ask the family if they would like to work together to fix it up.

The Autry family discovered a cemetery where many relatives were buried; unfortunately it was in bad shape -- completely overgrown with timber and brush. The family decided to make it their special project:

"We had enough family volunteers to completely clean and remove all the thick undergrowth from the one and one-half acre plot and set up all the fallen headstones -- all in one Saturday," says Milton Autry of Alabama. The Autry Family Association is also planning to do some fundraising to put a stone at the grave of a great-great-great grandfather.

Many families, while researching family lines, discover family graves which are unmarked or marked only by a rock. If these unmarked graves are of veterans you might want to contact the U.S. Department of Veterans Affairs (810 Vermont Avenue, NW, Washington, DC 20420) or your nearest VA Regional Office about a free headstone for the grave. You will need to request and fill out an Application for Standard Government Headstone or Marker for Installation in a Private or State Veterans' Cemetery (Form 40-1330). You must certify that the grave is an unmarked grave of a deceased veteran (a grave is considered marked if it has a monument which displays the decedent's name, date of birth, and date of death). A memorial headstone or marker can also be obtained to commemorate any veteran whose remains have not yet been recovered or identified, or were buried at sea.

Anne Ruisi of Alabama, who obtained a tombstone and a memorial marker for two ancestors who were Confederate soldiers advises, "It took a long time for the process -- usually six to eight months. I had to fill out a form requesting biographical info on the two soldiers, and supply proof of service in the form of service records."

The family of one of the two soldiers was very poor when he died in 1923, and no one ever knew where the other soldier had been buried; he died in a Chattanooga hospital early in the war.

The markers are free but it is up to the family to get them installed.

"Keep in mind how heavy these stones can be," says Anne. "Someone must accept delivery of them and the family arranges to have them placed at the grave."

Her family arranged a memorial service for the two ancestors in 1991. "We got a Civil War Confederate reenacting group, the 21st Alabama Inf., Co. D, to do the military honors. I am a reenactor and I dressed in my Sunday best dress to tell the family about these deceased southern patriots. A grandson of one of the soldiers led us in the Lord's Prayer, and the reenactors fired a 21 gun salute. It was very touching."

The reenactors did not charge a fee. "I don't know about Northern reenactors, but those in the South are 99% of the time pleased to serve as color guards, honor guards, etc. for a memorial service for any patriot, blue or gray," says Anne.

The Hamlett family in Virginia has made their private cemetery a family project all along; it was started in 1910 and family members are still maintaining it. Whenever surrounding brush threatens to encroach upon it the family gets together to work on it.

Some of the graves in the Hamlett cemetery were marked only by a rock, and the older generation who knew who was buried where and when were dying out. Family member Dorothy Foster began a project which would be worthwhile for many other families to work on:

"I started a book on the Hamlett Cemetery, drawing up a diagram of the gravesites, numbering them from the first to the thirty-third. Then I wanted to know something about that person," says Dorothy. The resulting book has photos, dates, and personal information about each of the people buried there: what kind of personality they had, what they did for a living, what they did for fun, who their children are, what caused their death, etc.

Along with the book, Dorothy and her brother worked on another project concerning the cemetery -- laying new grave markers for the unmarked graves, most of whom were infants. She paid the $40 apiece for them from the family cemetery fund but found that the next of kin for those graves were more than willing to reimburse the cost of the marble markers, happy that it had been done.

"One sister of an infant had never really known where her brother was buried," says Dorothy.

Photo 27: Courtesy of Dorothy Foster. Some members of the Hamlett family got together and built a 3- to 4-foot high rock wall around their private cemetery.

Photo 28: Courtesy of Dorothy Foster. When the original stone steps going over the wall became a problem for the older generation to climb, some of the younger generation worked together to replace the steps with a wrought iron gate.

Figure 86. Courtesy of Dorothy Foster. Diagram of gravesites at Hamlett Cemetery.

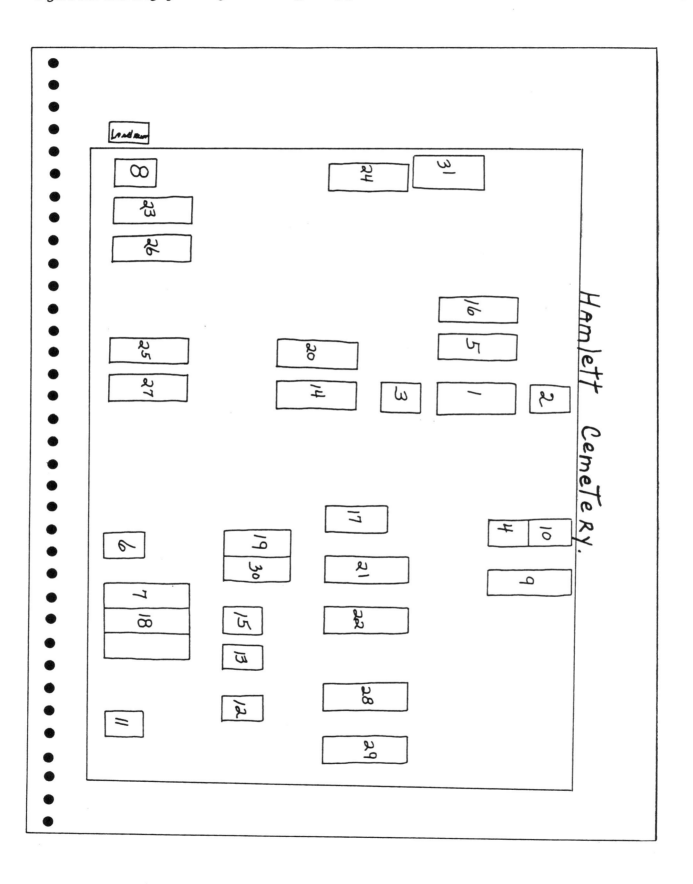

Figure 87. Courtesy of Dorothy Foster.
One page in the Hamlett Cemetery Booklet.

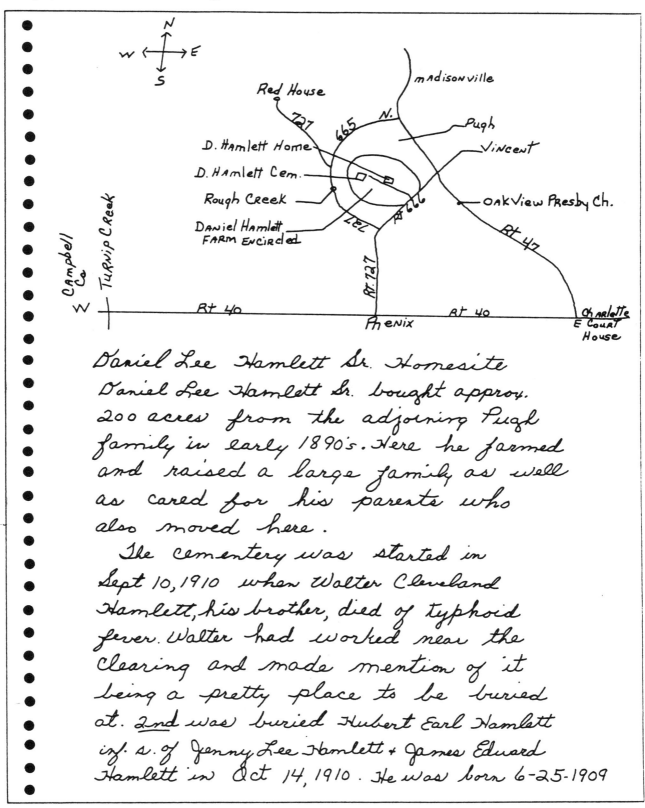

Daniel Lee Hamlett Sr. Homesite

Daniel Lee Hamlett Sr. bought approx. 200 acres from the adjoining Pugh family in early 1890's. Here he farmed and raised a large family as well as cared for his parents who also moved here.

The cementery was started in Sept 10, 1910 when Walter Cleveland Hamlett, his brother, died of typhoid fever. Walter had worked near the clearing and made mention of it being a pretty place to be buried at. 2nd was buried Hubert Earl Hamlett inf. s. of Jenny Lee Hamlett & James Edward Hamlett in Oct 14, 1910. He was born 6-25-1909

Some families may find that ancestors were buried in special plots on family land. If you want to check these you will need the permission of the current owner (plus, you don't want to unexpectedly encounter a bull in a pasture!). In some states the descendants of those people buried in a cemetery on private land have a right of access to the cemetery, subject to restrictions on when and how.

Many times you will find reference to an old family cemetery in a land deed, indicating that a cemetery was excluded when the land was sold such as "except the twelve foot square which the grantor reserves where two of his children are buried." Explore the soil with a thin probing rod since stones may be buried several inches to several feet.

Laws regarding access to and safeguarding cemeteries vary from state to state: "In North Carolina, for instance, it is a felony to knowingly desecrate any cemetery, " says Donna Flowers, the state coordinator for the North Carolina Cemetery Survey. "Therefore it is vital that a record of all graveyards be on file, usually in the county register of deeds' offices. This legal device may help protect cemeteries when land changes ownership. Another way to protect a cemetery is to make the community aware of its existence through publicity in the local newspaper."

Even if a cemetery does not need your family's physical help, it may need your financial help:

"The cemetery where many of our family are buried is not in perpetual care," says Mary Katherine Townsend of Texas. "We pay dues for our immediate family but there are several there who left no descendants -- other than nieces and nephews. So we 'pass the hat' at the Kelly Reunion to donate to keeping the cemetery mowed, etc."

Along with caring for the cemetery, your family might want to appoint a person or persons to attend to Memorial Day flowers. Roberta Mingyar's family has a committee for this:

"We always put flowers on the graves of Great Grandmother and Grandfather Himes, and Grandmother and Grandfather Shaffer," she says. "Both family reunions were started by these people."

One interesting activity to do during family reunions is to make a rubbing of a tombstone by placing a piece of paper over the stone and rubbing with the flat side of a crayon. Frame the best ones for wall hangings.

You might also want to preserve a record of tombstones (especially ones that are eroding) by photographing them. There are several methods for increasing the contrast of the lettering to the background so that the lettering is more readable in the photograph. One method is to rub flour into the engraving to highlight the letters, using a soft brush or folded paper towel to remove the flour around the letters. Another is to rub chalk on the flat surface of the gravestone, not the letters. A third method uses shaving cream; squirt it into the carved letters and use a styrofoam meat tray to scrape it off at surface level, leaving the foam in the indentations. Many times the engraving can be made more distinct by wetting the surface of the tombstone with a spray bottle of water. Be sure to bring a jug of water and a sponge to remove any chalk, flour, or shaving cream when you have finished.

If your family plans to get involved with the restoration of a family cemetery, you might want to join The Association for Gravestone Studies (30 Elm Street, Worcester, MA 01609). It is a non-profit international organization founded for the purpose of furthering the study and preservation of gravestones. Various AGS publications describe methods and techniques for recording cemetery data, restoring cemeteries and gravestones, photographing gravestones, and preparing legislation to protect gravestones from vandalism, theft, and demolition.

OTHER FAMILY PROJECTS

The Robinett Family Association of America is working to secure a "Robinett Room" in a new addition to the Westminster College Library. A minimum donation of $25,000 to the college is required, and the family is mounting a fund-raising effort for this project. The room will be a permanent repository for the bible of Allen Robinett, their immigrant ancestor, and other memorabilia.

Often, family members will join to buy a new organ, pulpit, or chair for the family church, given in memory of a deceased loved one. Many families have raised money to have their immigrant ancestor's name placed on The American Immigrant Wall of Honor on Ellis Island. The double-sided, semi-circular wall is a memorial to our nation's immigrant heritage. Names will be added for a limited time only; for more information contact The Statue of Liberty-Ellis Island Foundation, P.O. Box ELLIS, New York, NY 10163, (212) 883-1986.

Some families decide to donate heirlooms to historical societies and museums, where they can be better preserved and put on display. The John and Elizabeth Curtis/Curtiss Society donated a heirloom quilt to the Stratford Historical Society.

One expensive but exciting family project is to arrange a group tour to the country where your immigrant ancestors came from. This takes a great deal of work, money, and time, but imagine the thrill of walking through the streets of the little town in Europe where your great-great-great-grandfather once lived. A group of genealogists in one family began preparing for such a trip months in advance by placing an ad in that town's newspaper, requesting information from anyone who had knowledge of their ancestor. Not only did they get a reply, but a whole flock of distant relatives were waiting to welcome them to the town and show them the area!

Recreation Ideas

TALENT SHOW

A talent show is a regular feature of many family reunions. All ages can participate. When you send out notices about the reunion remind everyone that a talent show is planned and you would like at least one person from each family to have something prepared for it. Every family has talented individuals in its ranks and most have a ham or two who are just waiting for a little encouragement. It seems to be against some people's nature to volunteer to do anything (even people who enjoy performing), so don't be afraid to ask them to do what you know they do well.

Some of the best performances are those put together on the spur of the moment by two or more relatives who seldom see each other. In one family three male cousins who lived in Florida, Colorado, and Maine got together and performed a hilarious hula dance, complete with hula skirts made of strips of grocery sacks stapled to strings. The trio was such a hit that they have performed at each of the five reunions since then. A fourth cousin who is able to maintain a deadpan face despite the laughter from the audience gives an oral interpretation of the dance -- an ad lib fictitious story about the trials and tribulations of an ancestor.

Encourage the musicians and singers in the family. Suggest that others recite parody or original poems or compose a reunion rap song. Lip sync contests are always popular. If some family members enjoy writing ask if they would read aloud a selected piece of their work. Humorous pantomimes are always fun to perform and watch. Does anyone in your family perform magic tricks, ballet, or tap dancing?

Be sure to have a Master of Ceremonies who will introduce each act and pull the whole show together. Don't forget the talents of the youngest members of the family; everyone loves to watch a little group of preschoolers perform, whether it be a song or with rhythm instruments or whatever.

SKITS

Dramatize events in your family's past with skits; it could be a re-enactment of the day your immigrant ancestor set sail for America, or a fictionalized account of the day Grandpa first met Grandma (particularly appropriate for a reunion which is also celebration of their wedding anniversary). If there is an often-told story in the family which has several versions (depending on who is doing the telling!), performing a his-version-of-what-happened and her-version-of-what-happened pair of skits about it could be fun.

The relatives-turned-actors can memorize their lines if they wish, but another option which requires less preparation time and less nervousness about performing is to use a narrator. The narrator sits to the side of the stage area and reads the story, pausing every sentence or two while the actors act out that section of the story. This method is especially effective for a humorous skits and ones with small children.

The narrator can set the stage for the scene ("Once upon a time...") and can even interact with the actors as part of the skit. For instance, suppose you are doing a humorous skit about Grampa's first date with Grandma (which was a disaster from the moment he picked her up). Two grandchildren could be dressed appropriately to play the parts of the dating couple. The narrator describes how Grandpa accidentally hit Grandma in the nose and broke it; he then looks at the actor playing Grandpa and says, "Oh, Grandpa, I don't think this is going to be a case of love at first sight. Do you?" 'Grandpa' exaggerates a gloomy face and shakes his head no.

Skits do not necessarily have to deal with family history, nor be prepared beforehand. An entertaining, impromptu alternative is an activity called Create-A-Skit. Divide those people who wish to participate into groups with three to five people in each group, and have a bag containing five objects prepared in advance for each group. Draw numbers to determine by chance who gets which bag. Instruct each group to take their bag to a secluded area and prepare a skit which makes use of every person in the group and every item in the bag. The items do not, however, have to be used in the manner that they would normally be used. After a set amount of time the groups return and take turns performing. Be sure the audience is profuse with applause and encouragement.

Photo 29: Courtesy of Carolyn Cokerham. Narrator "Betsy Ross" tells about a well-known family incident while "George Washington" and ancestor "Uncle Jacob" act it out during this family reunion.

Costumes are not necessary but they can add to the fun. Browse at your local library for books on making costumes; one good book with ideas on how to make believable costumes from materials on hand is *Costumes for Plays and Playing* by Gail E. Haley (New York: Methuen; 1978). Here are some sources for patterns for historical clothing:

1. Amazon Vinegar and Pickling Works Drygoods
   2218 E. 11th Street
   Davenport, IA 52803
   (319) 322-6800
   (800) 798-7979
   FAX: (319) 322-4003

2. Past Patterns
   P.O. Box 7587
   Grand Rapids, MI 49510
   (616) 245-9456
   FAX (616) 241-4424

3. Richard The Thread
   8320 Melrose Ave., #201
   Los Angeles, CA 90069
   (213) 852-4997
   (800) 473-4997
   FAX: (213) 852-1604

4. Campbell's
   P.O. Box 400
   Gratz, PA 17030-0400
   (800 992-4406

SING-ALONG

Singing is a part of the family fun at the Bock Reunion: "One of our musically inclined relatives always brings her guitar, so there is a sing-along in the evening. The adults really enjoy the songs," says Sonia Cesarina.

What kinds of songs do your relatives enjoy singing: folk, country, religious, oldies-but-goodies? Include a songfest in your festivities. One suggestion: most families find that there is more and louder participation if you have printed copies of the words available for everyone. Two books to browse through for ideas for children's songs are *The Funny Song Book* by Esther L. Nelson (New York: Sterling Publishing Co., 1984), and *The Fireside Book of Fun and Game Songs* by Marie Winn and Allan Miller (New York: Simon and Schuster, 1974).

RECYCLING CONTEST

Photo 30: Use your imagination when creating costumes! This dress and the flowers and ribbon on the papier-maché hat are made entirely from plastic grocery bags.

Hold a costume contest and specify that all entries must be made entirely out of paper or plastic grocery sacks. Give everyone plenty of notice about the contest and encourage both adults and children to participate. The bags can be stitched, glued, taped, and/or stapled; crayons, felt markers, and/or paint can be used to add color. Don't forget the fashion accessories such as papier-mache shoes and frilly hats with ruffled plastic flowers!

Have contestants parade down a center aisle in their recycled creations for a fashion show so that the judges can make their decisions. Be as creative in your awards as the contestants have been with their designs: Best Overall Design, Best Use of Tape, Best Mother-Daughter matching outfits, Most Handsome and Elegant Male Creation, Scariest Costume, Best Mask, Best Use of Color, etc.

PARADE

Consider holding a reunion parade for the children. Lois Schafer's family did at their reunion. The children paraded one block down the street, holding balloons with the family name printed on them. "The kids loved it even though it lasted such a short time," she says. "It gave them something to remember."

HOMEMADE BOWLING GAMES

Kids of all ages love knocking down pins with a bowling ball, so set up a bowling alley at the reunion site -- in a driveway, on the slab floor of a pavilion, or on a tiled floor. It requires very little set-up time and little or no supervision -- a big plus for reunions with a shortage of volunteer help. Parents can watch from a distance while also visiting with other relatives.

Large diameter PVC pipe or 2x2s can be used as lane borders to keep the ball contained where you want it; use duct tape to hold the borders securely in place. A wood croquet ball makes a great bowling ball. Craft stores also have large diameter wood balls.

Wood spindle posts (from a home improvement store) can be used for one type of homemade bowling pin. Cut each post into two pins as shown in the photo. Paint as desired and finish with two coats of clear polyurethane for a durable finish. These pins will make that ever popular crashing sound as they fall! Hint: to make set up between players easier and faster, place small stickers or pieces of tape on the floor where each pin should stand. Young children who might have a hard time spacing the pins properly otherwise can easily set a pin on each sticker.

Photo 31: "Parts of wood spindle posts become Uncle Sam bowling pins with a little paint. Paint the coat blue, the striped pants red and white, and the hat black. A small white rectangle and a flesh-colored circle are painted on each side of the coat for a shirt cuff and hand."

Another option is papier-mache bowling pins. You can buy unpainted 9" tall forms at a craft store for about $1.70 each, or make them at home with flour-and-water glue and narrow strips of newspaper or paper grocery sacks. Use a rolled up newspaper (a little shorter than the desired finished height for the pin) for the center and build up the shape with paper strips dipped in glue. Allow the pins to dry after every two or three layers of paper. Paint white when finished.

Photo 32: "Personalized bowling pins are a big hit with the children."

For personalized bowling pins use photos of family members on them as shown in the photo. To do this, first have your local print shop make color copies of the photos you want to use (school photos are great for this). You can save money by taping as many photos as will fit on 8 1/2" x 11" sheets of paper before going to the print shop since you will be charged by the sheet -- whether there is one photo on it or four. Also, if the size of a face in a photograph is not large enough ask the print shop to enlarge it at the same time they make the color copy of it.

Use a transfer medium (such as Bond brand Lift Off) to transfer the photocopies to the papier-mache bowling pin. Follow directions on the bottle, applying the coats of liquid to an area a little larger than the head and neck. Carefully cut out the head and neck, soak in water, rub off the paper backing, and apply to bowling pin. Use black paint to outline the other body features (Fig. 88) and finish with two or more coats of clear polyurethane or acrylic spray. You may want to allow the children to play with this special bowling set during the reunion and use it as a door prize for one lucky child at the end of the festivities.

Figure 88. Body features on bowling pins.

TREASURE HUNT

These are great for any size family reunion and can be made more or less challenging to accommodate the participating age group. Although treasure hunts do require a considerable amount of preparation time they are well worth the effort. There's just something about searching for a treasure that brings out the kid in all of us!

Divide participants into teams of at least two and no more than five; any larger than this and usually two or three people end up having all the fun while the rest are dragged along behind. This game can be used to help get different branches of the family acquainted with each other by mixing up the aunts, uncles, and cousins on the teams. In order to involve the oldest members of the clan you might allow each team to choose one 'elder' to serve as their advisor. If the team doesn't know an answer to a question such as "What state was Grandma Betty born in?", perhaps the advisor will know.

Prepare and hide the clues ahead of time. The first clue -- which is handed out at the starting point -- indicates where to find the second clue. The second clue guides the team to the third clue, and so on to the final treasure. Decide where the hiding spot will be first and then compose a clue to lead the team there. Don't make the clues too easy; make them challenging!

All of the clues for each team's treasure hunt should have a letter and a number (A-1, A-2,...) in sequence. Draw letters from a bag to determine who gets which set of clues. Instruct everyone to always check any clues they find for their team's designated letter -- and to be a good sport! If one team accidentally finds a clue meant for another team, they must leave it EXACTLY where it was found.

The little containers for 35mm film are ideal for putting folded up clues in, especially if the treasure hunt will be held outdoors. These containers will protect the clues from moisture. Your local photography store will probably be glad to donate as many as you need. Little plastic bags could also be used.

Keep a master list of where all the clues are hidden in case any of the teams get stumped. Instead of having the teams find just clues, you might put a clue and part of a treasure map in each container. When all of the parts are found and pieced together they show the location of the treasure.

If you are running short on time for putting together this activity, the fill-in-the-blank form of clue is probably the easiest and fastest to compose. Use the same five beginning phrases or questions for each team and change only the ending instruction. Doing it this way also makes it easier to be sure that all sets of clues are equally difficult.

The treasures could be candy, a reunion souvenir such as a t-shirt or a tote bag with the family logo printed on it, or any number of things. Be sure all participants get something, along with a grand prize for the team that finishes first.

Example of a FILL IN THE BLANK clue using general information:

A. I'd rather see than be one.

$\overline{\quad}\ \overline{\quad}\ \overline{\quad}\ \overline{\quad}\ \overline{\quad}\ \overline{\quad}\ \overline{\quad}\qquad \overline{\quad}\ \overline{\quad}\ \overline{\quad}$
1 2 3 4 5 6 7   8 9 10

B. She ain't what she used to be.

11 12 13   14 15 16   17 18 19 20   21   22 23 24

C. Where is Death Valley?

25 26 27 28 29 30 31 32 33 34

D. Do-see-do means

35 36 37 38   39 40   41 42 43 44

E. The person who died twice in the bible.

$\overline{}\ \overline{}\ \overline{}\ \overline{}\ \overline{}\ \overline{}\ \overline{}$
45 46 47 48 49 50 51

THE NEXT CLUE IS $\overline{}\ \overline{}$ $\overline{}\ \overline{}\ \overline{}$ $\overline{}\ \overline{}\ \overline{}\ \overline{}\ \overline{}$
                      28 32   11 12 7   39 12 33 4 16

$\overline{}\ \overline{}\ \overline{}\ \overline{}$ $\overline{}\ \overline{}$ $\overline{}\ \overline{}\ \overline{}$ $\overline{}\ \overline{}\ \overline{}\ \overline{}\ \overline{}$
35 9 40 44   14 32   39 12 24   11 12 28 23 16

$\overline{}\ \overline{}\ \overline{}\ \overline{}\ \overline{}$.
51 12 13 6 29

     (answer: a purple cow
                 the old gray mare
                 California
                 back to back
                 Lazarus
                 IN THE THIRD BOOK ON THE THIRD SHELF)

Note: Don't tell them everything. Let them figure out where on the premises to find books on a third shelf.

To make the Treasure Hunt quizzes equally difficult for each team, try using the same beginning five phrases or questions but different ending instructions. For instance, the final line for Team #2 might be:

FOR THE NEXT CLUE LOOK $\overline{}\ \overline{}\ \overline{}\ \overline{}\ \overline{}\ \overline{}\ \overline{}\ \overline{}\ \overline{}\ \overline{}$
                               50 32 16 7 4 32 13 1 39 12

$\overline{}\ \overline{}\ \overline{}$ $\overline{}\ \overline{}\ \overline{}\ \overline{}\ \overline{}\ \overline{}$ $\overline{}\ \overline{}\ \overline{}\ \overline{}\ \overline{}\ \overline{}\ \overline{}\ \overline{}$.
11 12 24   21 19 32 3 49 13   51 5 31 24 48 16 24 4

(answer: UNDERNEATH THE MANURE SPREADER. This could be fun to watch if no one on that team knows what a manure spreader is or where to find it on the farm!)

Another example of a FILL IN THE BLANK type clue:
A. Fibber McGee and
b $\overline{}\ \overline{}\ \overline{}\ \overline{}\ \overline{}$
   1 2 3 4 5

B. Perry Mason's creator.

   $\overline{}\ \overline{}\ \overline{}\ \overline{}$ $\overline{}\ \overline{}\ \overline{}\ \overline{}\ \overline{}\ \overline{}\ \overline{}$ $\overline{}\ \overline{}\ \overline{}\ \overline{}\ \overline{}\ \overline{}\ \overline{}$
   6 7 8 9   10 11 12 13 14 15 16   17 18 19 20 21 22 23

C. What Jack cracked.

   $\overline{}\ \overline{}\ \overline{}$ $\overline{}\ \overline{}\ \overline{}\ \overline{}\ \overline{}$
   24 25 26   27 28 29 30 31

D. Where Peter stashed his wife.

   $\overline{}\ \overline{}\ \overline{}\ \overline{}\ \overline{}\ \overline{}\ \overline{}$ $\overline{}\ \overline{}\ \overline{}\ \overline{}\ \overline{}$
   32 33 34 35 36 37 38   39 40 41 42 43

E. Where Rebecca lived.

   $\overline{}\ \overline{}\ \overline{}\ \overline{}\ \overline{}\ \overline{}\ \overline{}\ \overline{}\ \overline{}\ \overline{}$ $\overline{}\ \overline{}\ \overline{}\ \overline{}$
   44 45 46 47 48 49 50 51 52 53   54 55 56 57

LOOK $\overline{25}\ \overline{13}$ $\overline{11}\ \overline{24}\ \overline{6}$ $\overline{54}\ \overline{37}\ \overline{7}\ \overline{10}\ \overline{11}$ $\overline{11}\ \overline{19}\ \overline{9}\ \overline{15}$

$\overline{39}\ \overline{29}\ \overline{33}\ \overline{11}\ \overline{40}$ $\overline{51}\ \overline{54}$ $\overline{11}\ \overline{40}\ \overline{41}$ $\overline{44}\ \overline{25}\ \overline{20}\ \overline{6}\ \overline{30}\ \overline{55}\ \overline{43}\ \overline{36}$

(answer: Molly
  Erle Stanley Gardner
  his crown
  pumpkin shell
  Sunnybrook Farm
  IN THE FIRST TREE SOUTH OF THE SIDEWALK)

Example of a FILL IN THE BLANK clue using family information:
A. What was the first name of Grampa Benjamin's mother?

$\overline{1}\ \overline{2}\ \overline{3}\ \overline{4}\ \overline{5}\ \overline{6}\ \overline{7}\ \overline{8}\ \overline{9}$

B. How many children did Robert and Shana have?

$\overline{10}\ \overline{11}\ \overline{12}\ \overline{13}\ \overline{14}$

C. What was Grandma Emily's profession?

$\overline{15}\ \overline{16}\ \overline{17}\ \overline{18}\ \overline{19}\ \overline{20}$
bb
D. What was Grampa's favorite dog's name?

$\overline{21}\ \overline{22}\ \overline{23}\ \overline{24}\ \overline{25}$

E. What state was Grandma born in?

$\overline{26}\ \overline{27}\ \overline{28}\ \overline{29}\ \overline{30}\ \overline{31}\ \overline{32}\ \overline{33}$

FOR YOUR NEXT CLUE, $\overline{12}\ \overline{20}\ \overline{2}\ \overline{24}\ \overline{25}\ \overline{16}$

$\overline{7}\ \overline{15}\ \overline{27}\ \overline{29}\ \overline{31}\ \overline{14}\ \overline{3}\ \overline{5}$ $\overline{21}\ \overline{23}\ \overline{30}\ \overline{10}$ $\overline{22}\ \overline{9}\ \overline{33}$ $\overline{32}\ \overline{14}$

(answer: Bathsheba
  eight
  lawyer
  Champ
  Illinois
  GRAMPA ELLIOTTS CANE HAS IT
(The clue could be folded into a narrow strip and taped to his cane in an inconspicuous spot. If the cane is black, cover the clue with a piece of black construction paper or black electrical tape to make it blend in.)

Example of a clue using an A = 1 code:
"6-15-21-18"
is the answer to 2 + 2.
Continue that thought and you'll discover
the location of the next clue.
 12-15-15-11
 1-2-15-22-5
 20-8-5
 3-15-1-20
 3-12-15-19-5-20
 4-15-15-18
(answer: LOOK ABOVE THE COAT CLOSET
DOOR)

Another example:
If A=1
it's up to you
to decipher where
we've hidden Clue Two.
 12-15-15-11
 21-14-4-5-18
 1
 18-15-3-11
 2-5-8-9-14-4
 20-8-5
 2-1-18-14
(answer: LOOK UNDER A ROCK BEHIND THE
BARN)

Another example:
The numbers go to twenty-six
(and that should ring a bell!).
Where is the treasure hidden?
The numbers below will tell.
 9-14
 1
 2-18-15-23-14
 19-1-3-11
 9-14
 7-18-1-14-4-13-1
 12-21-3-9-12-12-5-19
 3-1-8
(answer: IN A BROWN SACK IN GRANDMA
 LUCILLES CAR)

Example of a riddle clue:
Sometimes I'm high.
Sometimes I'm low.
Sometimes I'm fast.
Sometimes I'm slow.
Bottoms often rest on top.
Your clue now is taped below.
(answer: the bottom of the swing seat)

Another example:
What do you find when PETS goes
backward?
Two don't count; you must press onward.
Find a spot where seven's the number.
Count to three and then look under.
(answer: PETS spelled backward is STEP. The
ones in front of the house don't count
because there's only two of them. The cellar
has seven steps. When the team descends
to the third step they will see a can of paint;
under it is the clue.)

Another example:
It has a tongue but cannot eat;
The one you want belongs to Pete.
Ask him nicely. Be specific.
With his help you'll do terrific!
(answer: The clue has been hidden inside
Uncle Pete's shoe -- with his permission of
course. He has been instructed not to let a
Treasure Hunt team have it unless they ask
specifically for a shoe.)

SCAVENGER HUNT

Scavenger hunts can be done in teams or with individual players. Each person or team is given a list of items to find, boundaries of the area to look for the items, and a time limit. The person or team who finds the largest amount of items on the list in the shortest time is the winner.

There are several types of scavenger hunts. Young children will enjoy searching for specific things such as an acorn, an interesting rock, a feather, etc. while on a nature walk with an adult leader. Supply each child with a little bag to put the 'treasures' in.

A genealogy scavenger hunt can be a lot of fun at a cemetery. Prepare a list of information that can be found on the gravestones there: find a person who died on January 21, 1889; find a person who has a squirrel on their tombstone; what is the name of the Anderson who was "...beloved by each of his three wives", etc.

Living people are the object of the Scavenger Hunts at the Himes-Shaffer Family Reunions. According to Roberta Mingyar of West Virginia each person is given a list of descriptions such as someone wearing red socks, someone with a bald head, someone wearing a class ring, etc. When you find someone matching the description they sign your list. "If the person signs that he or she can stand on their head they have to prove it," says Roberta.

Another interesting type of scavenger hunt is a Photo Scavenger Hunt. The participants are divided into teams. Each team is given a loaded instamatic camera, a list of things they must photograph, and a set time to be back at the starting point. The list could include these types of things: a photo of six members of the team inside a phone booth with the door closed, a photo of four members of the team standing on their heads at the same time, a people pyramid at least three people tall, etc.

TRUE OR FALSE GAME

Compose a list of twenty statements about members of the family, such as "Grandpa Howard was a cross-country runner when he was in high school." Some of the statements should be true and some should be false. Teams or individual players try to determine which are which and are awarded a point each time they are correct. Be sure everyone knows which were true and which were false at the end of the game so that mis-information doesn't end up passed around the family!

GUESS WHO? AUTOBIOGRAPHY GAME

Give each person two sheets of paper and a pencil. On one sheet each person should write their name and a paragraph about an incident in their lives. When everyone has finished, collect these paragraphs and shuffle the sheets so that they are in no particular order. The game leader reads each paragraph aloud; everyone else writes down on the other sheet who they think the author is. The person with the most correct answers wins. NOTE: Don't hurry this game along; the conversation that inevitably follows the reading of each paragraph is half the fun!

FAMILY QUIZ

The Himes-Shaffer Reunion organizers put together a How Well Do You Know Your Family? quiz in case they needed additional activities for a rainy day. Here are some of the questions included in the quiz for their sixty-first reunion:
1. What was Grandma Himes' maiden name?
2. Can you name all of Uncle John Himes' children?
3. Who makes looms for weaving?
4. Who is the vice president of this year's reunion?
5. Who got married on horseback?
6. Who owns a bakery?
Test your own family's knowledge of past and present relatives!

ART SHOW FOR THE CHILDREN

Fix up a separate area or room with tables and plenty of supplies so that the children can create paintings, drawings, clay sculptures -- whatever form of art appeals to them. You could suggest a theme such as ancestors on the move: on the boat crossing the ocean, in covered wagons crossing the plains, etc. When the children are finished and have helped clean up the area, create an art gallery to display their talents. Drape an oatmeal box with fabric for a pedestal to show off a piece of clay sculpture. Make construction paper frames for the paintings and drawings. Each piece of artwork should have a tag with the name of the young artist.

When everything is ready, instruct the youngsters to escort the rest of the family to the grand opening of the exhibit. You might want to hold an awards ceremony (with a certificate of appreciation for the contribution of each young artist to family art) and serve cookies and punch. This is the stuff wonderful childhood memories about family reunions are made of!

HOMEMADE MOVIES

Many families are paying to have all their reels of home movies copied onto a video tape; here's a way to do it yourself, end up with something extra on the tape that a business couldn't add, and have fun at a family reunion in the process. Set up the old movie projector and screen in a comfortable area where everyone can sit and watch. Then, set up a camcorder to record what is being shown on the screen. The advantage to this is that when people watch old, silent home movies there is usually a lot of reminiscing going on about what they are seeing. Your camcorder will record this conversation as well as the picture, making the resulting tape much more meaningful and precious than one with the background music many companies will add to your movies when they copy them. NOTE: You will probably get many requests for copies of this tape. Why not calculate how much it will cost you (including packaging and postage) and add a little extra, informing everyone that the extra money raised will be added to the reunion fund to pay for next year's reunion.

Don't forget to create some new home movies during the reunion. If you have a bunch of outgoing teens attending, give them a camcorder to use and challenge them to create an interesting tape that deals with something about the family or the reunion. Give them a deadline to meet, such as the beginning of the two o'clock entertainment program the next day. Play the tape for everyone during the program.

SQUARE DANCING

Consider hiring a square dance caller for an evening. It's fun for all ages, good exercise, and isn't that hard to learn -- at least the simpler steps, that is! If someone in the family belongs to a square dance group, ask if the group would be willing to come to the reunion site and put on a demonstration for everyone.

FAMILY OLYMPICS

Divide the family into teams and hold a Funtastic Family Olympics! The games could take place during one hour on one day, or it could be a week-long contest with new competitions each day and the points earned totaled on the final day. Having medallions, ribbons, or trophies to award at the end will greatly add to the enjoyment. Use a large piece of posterboard or foam-core board to publicly record the results of each event; this enhances team spirits!

Since many people do not attend the whole reunion (especially those which last three to seven days) it is best to form teams in a way which will allow latecomers the opportunity to participate and not make those who must leave early feel guilty. One way to accomplish this is to set up the teams as a category of persons, such as cousins versus aunts and uncles; each team then decides who will compete for their team at each event. For instance, a tricycle riding relay might require four people from each team and a family quiz competition might require three. Obviously each person on a team will have things he does well and things he doesn't do so well. The team tries to chose the best people for each event, but also makes sure everyone gets a chance to compete. The job of those teammates not competing in the current event is to cheer on those who are competing. Make sure the rules of good sportsmanship are observed; no booing or dirty tricks.

Include a variety of events which require many different abilities. A family quiz will require knowledge of facts about the family, so older people in the family will probably have an advantage. Young children will probably have an advantage in a tricycle relay (just watching an adult try to ride one can be hilarious!). Athletic teenagers will have the advantage in a obstacle course race. Browse through this chapter for ideas for competitions.

RELAYS

Team relay games are great for promoting togetherness, something all families need. Try these relays or make up some more of your own:

1. Balloon Sweep Relay

   At the starting signal the first person in each team's line uses a broom to sweep a balloon around a specified goal (such as a bucket) and back to the starting line. He hands the broom to the next team member, and so on. The first team done wins. If the balloon busts, that team member must return to the starting line, get another balloon, and start over. If you will be playing this outside on a windy day try putting a couple of tablespoons of water in the balloon before blowing it up. This will weigh it down enough to keep it from blowing away.

2. Balloon Pop Relay

   The teams stand in rows at the starting line, with each person holding a balloon. At the signal to start the first person in each line runs to a specified chair, pops the balloon by sitting on it, and runs back to the starting line. He tags the next team member to let him go. The first team with all balloons popped wins. For added difficulty you could make them run under a table on the way to the chair.

3. Shoebox Shuffle

   Supply each team with two large shoeboxes. The teams line up at the starting line and when the starting signal is given the first person in each line steps into the shoeboxes, shuffles up to and around a specified goal (such as a bucket), and shuffles back to the next teammate. That person steps into the shoeboxes, and so on. The first team finished wins.

4. Crazy Cane Relay

   Line the teams up at a starting line and give the first person in each line a cane or long stick. At the starting signal he or she takes the cane to a goal (such as a circle of masking tape on the floor) a few feet away and places one end of the cane in the center of goal. Both hands are placed over the upper end of the cane and the forehead is rested on top of the hands. In this position and with eyes closed the person walks around the cane three times, stands up, counts to five, and takes the cane to the next team member. This isn't as easy as it sounds.

5. Balloon Race Relay

   Divide into equal teams. You will need two goal lines several yards apart. Have half of each team line up behind one goal line, and the other half line up behind the other goal line. Give the first person of each team at one goal line a balloon. At the starting signal each person with a balloon tosses it into the air and continues to keep it in the air by tapping it, all the while trying to get it to a teammate on the other goal line. That teammate must make his first tap on the balloon while his feet are still on the goal line; he bats it back across to another teammate on the first goal line. The game continues until each person on the team has traveled with the balloon.

6. Rolling Relay

   The object of this relay is to roll something to a goal and back to the next team member. You could roll a tire with your hands, a lemon with a pencil, or a marble with a stick, etc.

7. Tricycle Relay

   This is a lot of fun to watch and the younger children will get a kick out of seeing an adult trying to operate a little tricycle. Borrow enough tricycles so that each team has one. Each team member takes a turn riding the tricycle to a goal point and back.

8. Egg in a Teaspoon Relay

Each person on each team has a spoon; the first person in line also has an egg. The object of the relay is to carry an egg in the spoon to a specified goal line and back to the next player. The egg has to be passed to the next person's teaspoon without anyone touching it with their hands. If the egg falls at any time, the person must go back to the starting line and begin again.

A fun extra for this game would be to paint the face and name of a relative on each egg and label the goal line with the name of the country your immigrant ancestor came from. Tell everyone they are going to take their relatives for a trip back to the old country and you hope they'll take good care of them during the trip!

PASSING-DOWN-THE-LINE TEAM RACES

1. Lifesaver Candy Relay

Divide into equal teams. Teammates stand in a straight line. Each person has a toothpick in their mouth and their hands behind their back. The object of the game is to see which team can pass a candy Lifesaver from toothpick to toothpick to the end of the line first. If the candy drops on the floor or anyone uses their hands the team must start over.

2. "Necking"

The teams stand in lines as before, but the object this time is to pass an orange down the line using only chins and necks.

3. Bucket Brigade

Divide into teams and have each team stand in a line. Place a bottle of water on one end of each team and an empty bottle on the other end. (Note: use identical bottles.) Each person is given a paper cup. When the starting signal is given the team member next to the bottle of water fills his cup with water, pours the water into the cup of the next person, and so on down the line until the last person in line pours the water into the empty bottle.

The object is to be fast but careful. Award one point to the team that finishes first and two points to the team with the most water in the second bottle. If you are playing with only two teams it is fun to have them stand back to back and allow them to jostle each other as the water is being poured from cup to cup.

4. Through The Loop

Team members stand in a line and connect by holding hands. A large circle of rope lays on the floor in front of the first person on each team. At the starting signal he picks up the rope with his free hand and maneuvers his body through the rope. The first team to get the rope all the way through the line (without letting go of hands) and laying on the floor at the end of the line wins.

BALLOON FUN

Balloons are inexpensive and colorful, and you can stick the equipment necessary for a whole afternoon of fun in your back pocket! Give the following ideas a try:

1. Stomp The Balloon

This activity requires a large area. Attach 1 1/2' to 2' long strings to each balloon and tie a balloon to one ankle of each person. The object is to bust everyone else's balloons by stomping on them while keeping your own intact. The person with the last surviving balloon wins. (Note: sometimes the game is played by attaching the balloons to the waist so that the balloon is a tail. Give each person a 'balloon smasher' made from a rolled up newspaper.)

The game can be played in teams by assigning a different color of balloons to each team. Everyone begins stomping when the starting whistle is blown, and stops when the whistle is blown again. The team with the most balloons remaining intact wins.

2. Water Balloon Battle

Fill balloons with water and stockpile an equal number of them for each team. The teams have a chance to throw balloons at each other for a set length of time, after which all the other relatives vote for the winner -- the driest team! A great game on really hot summer days.

3. Balloon Shaving Contest

Kids love this contest. Draw faces on inflated balloons with a waterproof marker and identify them with names of male members of the family: Grampa John, Uncle Henry, etc. Cut a pair of feet for each balloon out of sponge or corrugated cardboard; punch a hole in the center of the feet and pull the balloon stem and knot through the hole for a base. Spread shaving lotion on each face and see who can shave their balloon the fastest -- without busting the balloon! It is preferable to hold this activity outdoors because it can be quite messy.

4. Balloon Release

Rent a helium tank from a party supply store. Have each person write the following on a small piece of paper:

> This balloon was part of the festivities at the (surname) Family Reunion.
> Our family wishes your family many happy gatherings. Please notify
> (name of person) at (address) to let us know our greetings have been
> received!

Inflate the balloons with helium and attach a string to each one. The release of all of the balloons in unison can be a nice climax for your reunion program, perhaps immediately after a closing prayer.

BINGO

Bingo is popular at many family reunions. Players have cards with random numbers printed in a group of squares -- five squares down and five squares across. Numbers are drawn randomly and called out. Anyone with that number on their card puts a marker on that square. The first person to have markers on five squares in a row (across, down, or diagonally) and yell "Bingo!" wins a prize. Any small items such as pebbles or uncooked beans can be used as markers.

The Colburn Reunion always includes a bingo game on Saturday evening following a cookout together:

"For prizes each family has to bring three homemade items for each member in their family," says Jo Ann Casebier of Kansas.

Roberta Mingyar's daughter created some living gifts for her donation to the prize table at their reunion. She repotted many 'babies' from a spider plant, put them in small white paper cups, cut out white eyes, put in black centers for the eyes, and stuck them on a leaf. Bingo winners choose a prize from anything on the donation table.

One version of this game, Hello Bingo, is a good ice breaker to play at the beginning of the reunion. Draw a Bingo sheet as shown in Fig. 89 and pass out a copy to each person. Instruct them to ask a different relative to sign each square (they may want to print the person's name above the signature if it is difficult to read). The name of each person present is written on separate strips of paper and placed in a container. Names are drawn at random and the first person to mark five in a row wins.

HUMAN TIC-TAC-TOE

Here's a fun version of an old childhood game. Line up nine chairs or nine pieces of paper (taped to the floor) in a three-by-three square formation. Two teams play, one on each side of the formation. The team captains takes turns calling out the name of a teammate and directing which space he should occupy. The object is for one team to get three players in a row (across, down, or diagonally) before the other team does.

You will need a way to identify one team from the other. You could make sashes from two different colors of disposable plastic tablecloths for the team members to tie around the waist, or have everyone on one team take off their shoes.

Figure 89

Figure 89. The squares must be large enough for signatures.

WILSON FAMILY BINGO

		FREE		

LIZARD'S TAIL

Divide into two or more groups. Each group forms a line with each person holding onto the waist of the person in front of him. The last person in each line has a tail (handkerchief) partially tucked into his back pocket or waistband. The object is for the first person in each line to snatch another line's tail; the rest of the team members must continue holding onto the waist of the person in front of them at all times. If your 'lizard' loses its tail the first person in line goes to the back of the line and the game begins again. Give everyone a chance to be a head and a tail.

STACKING CONTEST

At first glance this seems to be a game for young children, but you will probably find adults testing their skills at this game too! The object is simply to see who can built the highest tower. You can use any number of things for the objects to be stacked: wooden beads, film canisters, yogurt containers, coffee cans, etc. If possible collect enough of them so that two people can try it at the same time. The more noise the items make when the tower crashes, the more fun it is!

REUNION RESCUE

Divide into teams with five people on each team. Give each team a blanket which is big enough and strong enough to carry a person on. One person on each team is chosen to be the victim. The victims all go out to a specified area several yards away from the starting line and lie down. When the starting signal is given the remaining four people on each team run to the victim, spread out the blanket, and place the victim on the blanket. Each teammate grabs a corner of the blanket and they all head for the starting line. The first team to cross the line wins.

SPELLING RELAY

Cut poster board into squares approximately 5" x 5". Use large black markers to print a letter of the alphabet on each card, making two complete alphabet sets for each team. The teams stand behind a starting line. The cards for each team are placed on a chair or table several yards away.

Prepare a list of words (or perhaps names of ancestors) in advance to make sure there are enough letters in each set of cards to spell them one at a time. The game leader tells everyone how many letters will be in the word; if it has five letters the first five people in each line should get ready to run. When the leader announces the word those five people run to their set of cards and find the appropriate ones -- one card per person. The first team to face the starting line in the proper order to spell out the word wins that round. These players then go to the end of the line and another round is played with the next teammates in line.

JUMP THE CREEK

Place two sticks on the ground parallel to each other and about two feet apart. Everyone who wants to participate lines up behind the sticks and jumps across. Move the sticks further apart after each round of jumping. Anyone who cannot make the jump is eliminated. Continue until only one the champion jumper is left. Note: make sure there are no sharp stubs on the sticks that could injure a child if he falls.

RAW EGG TOSS

Have the players form two lines, with each player in the first line holding a raw egg and facing a partner in the second line. At the signal he tosses the egg to his partner. Any couple who breaks their egg is eliminated. The players take a step backward and toss the egg again. Continue until only one couple remains with their egg intact.

BABY PICTURE CONTEST

Ask each person to bring a baby picture of himself or herself to the reunion. Display the photos and have everyone guess who is who. (You might want to post an alphabetical list of the names of everyone included in the display.) The person who correctly identifies the most photographs wins a prize.

RACES

Each race involves a starting and finish line. When the starting signal is given, the contestants race from the starting line to the finish line. The first to reach the finish line is the winner.

1. Three-legged Races
   Partners stand side by side and tie their two center legs together for this race. Teamwork is required to hobble to the finish line on the resulting three legs.

2. Sack Race
   Each person steps into a gunny sack at the starting line and hops to the finish line. If there are a lot of contestants and a limited number of sacks available you could have four (or more) people compete in each race and then have the winners of each race compete again for the championship.

3. Backward Race
   Divide into teams and have them line up behind the starting line. The first person on each team gets down on hands and knees. At the sound of the starting signal he races -- backwards -- to the finish line. The first person there wins a point for his team. Repeat until each person on each team has raced. The team with the most points wins.

4. Double Racers
   Contestants work as partners, standing back to back with arms interlocked. The first pair to reach the finish line wins.
   This can also be played in teams as a relay. Members on each team race in pairs to a goal line and back. The next pair can take off as soon as the first pair tags them. The first team to finish wins.

5. Balloon Race
   Contestants race to the finish line with a water balloon held between their knees. If they touch the balloon with their hands or it touches the ground they must go back to the starting line and begin again.

SQUIRT GUNS

You can have a lot of fun with squirt guns on a hot summer day! Besides the obvious of seeing who can get who the wettest, you can play games such as a water gun shooting gallery. The target is lighted candles, and the object is to see who can put out the flame with the fewest number of squirts. Supervise this game closely and don't leave the candles laying around afterward; a child might decide to hold a private version of the contest later.

Another game is played by having each person hold a squirt gun in one hand and one of their ankles in the other. It is best if two to five people play at a time. They begin in a close circle with their backs to each other. When the starting signal is given the water gun battle begins. Anyone who lets go of their ankle or falls down is out of the game. Players will find that they must use strategy to conserve water.

BARNYARD

Play this game indoors in a room that can be darkened by turning off the lights. Write the names of animals which are easy to mimic (frog, dog, cow) on pieces of paper -- one piece of paper for each person playing, and have an equal number of each animal. Mix the papers up and randomly give one to each player. Everyone should sit on the floor and silently look to see what animal they have. Tell everyone how many of each type of animal there should be and turn off the lights. The players stand and shuffle around the room while making the sound of their animal. When two players of the same species find each other they join hands and continue making the sound to locate the rest of the group. The group which is first to find everyone and call out "The barn is full!" is the winner.

PITCHING GAMES

Children love pitching games. Here are four to try:

1. Make a beanbag toss game with dried beans and odd socks which lost their mate on wash day. Put about 1/2 cup of beans in each sock and tie a knot in the middle of it. The children try to toss the socks in a box or laundry basket located a few feet away.

2. Bounce super balls into a basket a few feet away. Even the teenagers won't be able to resist showing off their skills on this game! The ball must bounce on the floor at least once before going in the basket. Make sure you set up the game in a location where the balls won't be bouncing their way onto the heads of other relatives who are trying to converse with each other, or into a table full of food. After the kids have practiced for a while hold a contest in which each person gets ten tries at bouncing the ball into the basket. Present an award or prize to the person who gets the most in. (Don't forget to have a piece of posterboard and marker to prominently display everyone's score!)

3. Nail a number of different sized tin cans to a board, with open ends tilting out. Each can is given a different number value. Points are earned by tossing bottle caps (or pennies or slugs) into the cans. The children play to see who can accumulate the most points with five bottlecaps. Or, set it up so that the children choose a prize from one of three or four boxes; each box has a range of points printed on it. The smaller children will need help figuring out what their score is. Ask a couple of teenage cousins to be in charge of this game.
   If there is an artist in the family, ask if they would draw some faces on the board. Ten points could be earned by feeding Great Grandpa, five points for feeding Uncle Henry, and so on.

4. This is a Pitch-Until-You-Win game, popular because everyone is a winner. Fill small plastic or paper bags with little trinkets, party favors, and/or candy. String a rope between two heavy chairs or a couple of trees, and hang the bags on it with clothespins. Give the player a handful of rings (these could be cardboard rings, rings made from wire, rubber jar rings used for canning, etc.). Each player keeps on tossing rings until he rings a clothespin, at which time he gets to have what is inside that bag.
   The game is more fun if you do not make the contents of each bag identical; this way either the child will be aiming for a specific bag if he can see what is in each one, or else the contents will be a surprise if the bags are not see-through. Having two children toss rings at the same time also adds to the enjoyment of the game; each wants to see who will be the first to ring a bag!

ROAD RALLY

Road rallies require a lot of time to prepare and check (and double-check) for mistakes, but everyone ought to experience the fun and challenge of being in one at least once in their life!
   Divide relatives who want to participate into teams of at least two (one must have a driver's license and a car available) but no more than four. Each team is given identical instructions which will lead them on a course around roads in the local area (preferably a rural area). The teams draw numbers to determine the order they will leave the starting point in and a judge will send the cars out at three minute intervals. This prevents one team from just following the car ahead.
   An example of a road rally rules and instruction sheet is shown in Fig. 90. Two people who were not involved in laying out the course should make a test run to see if there are any mistakes in the instructions. Make any corrections and have another team (ask your neighbors and friends for help!) double-check the course before having copies made of the instruction sheet. Pass out the

instruction sheets a few minutes before the start of the rally so that you can answer any general questions teams might have. Make sure each team has a pen or pencil.

Figure 90

CHRISTENSON FAMILY REUNION ROAD RALLY
RULES:

Follow the instructions given below. Dirt roads (with no gravel) and private driveways should not be considered when deciding how to follow the directions. Don't forget to answer the questions; the answers aren't always obvious, but they are on the course. A point system will be used to determine the 1st, 2nd, and 3rd place winners. Points will be awarded for correct mileage, correct time, and correct answers. Points will be deducted for incorrect mileage and for coming in early or late. The correct time is based on the posted speed limits. If you do not see a posted speed limit, assume it to be 40 m.p.h. The judges will record your start and finish time and mileage. The number of blanks at the end of each question indicate how many words are required in the answer If you get lost or have been out more than 1 1/2 hours return immediately to the starting point. If you get lost, stop and ask directions to John Christenson's farm on the Bluemound Road or call us at _____ and we will tell you how to get back here. IMPORTANT: **DRIVE SAFELY**. USE COMMON SENSE AND CAUTION. ANY TEAM INVOLVED IN AN ACCIDENT IS AUTOMATICALLY DISQUALIFIED. ******HAVE FUN!******

DIRECTIONS:

1. Left at T.

2. Turn right at first opportunity.

What color is the first barn after turning on your right? _____

3. After bridge, take first left.

4. Turn left at three silos.

What is Mr. Anderson's first name? _____

What color is 'Jess and Verna's' mailbox? _____

5. Turn left at first stop sign.

6. Turn right after the fourteenth house on the left.

What is the name of the creek? _____ _____

7. Left at T.

What is the fine for littering? _____

8. Right at second opportunity.

What is the full name of the Cemetery?_____ _____ _____

Points are scored on the basis of time, mileage, and correct answers to the questions. A test run of the course by someone who already knows it will determine exactly how many miles it is long and how much time it should take if speed limits are followed and the correct turns are made. Award points for correct time, correct mileage, and correct answers. Deduct points for incorrect mileage, minutes early, or minutes late. This means that the judge at the starting/finish line needs to record starting and finish times and mileages for each team. Be prepared with additional questions about things along the course in case there is a tie.

FISHING GAMES

Young children will find this game very enjoyable. Buy artificial apples from a craft store; attach a loop of thin wire to the stem and paint a number on the bottom of each apple. Float the apples in a child's wading pool filled with water. Make a fishing pole with a stick or bamboo pole (not too long for the little tykes), string, and a 'hook' made from a curved piece of stiff wire.

Have at least three different boxes containing prizes; the number painted on the bottom of the apple the child catches determines from which box the child chooses a prize. For instance, numbers 1 through 9 choose from box 1, numbers 10 through 19 choose from box 2, and so on. If there are older relatives present who prefer to sit and watch activities instead of participating, ask if they would be willing to handle the prize boxes. When a child brings them an apple, they check the number and tell the youngster which box to choose from.

Note: You could paint the name and year of the reunion on the apples and give them away as Christmas tree ornaments for door prizes later.

PROGRESSIVE PICTURE

All the children should be sitting in a circle around a table for this activity; give each child a piece of blank paper and crayons or a pencil. Tell them that they are going to draw a picture of a beautiful park, and to start by drawing a tree in the park. When everyone has drawn a tree, have them pass their paper to the person on their right. Something else which is found in a park (bird, picnic table, plate on the picnic table, etc.) is announced, drawn, and the papers are passed to the right again. This is repeated until each paper has made its way all the way around the table and is back to the original owner. The children get a kick out of seeing the resulting picture which all their cousins have helped draw.

Instead of a park you might want to draw a picture of something pertaining to the family, such as Grandma's kitchen or an uncle's farm.

COMPOSITE PICTURE

This is another drawing activity for children, but they make one big picture out of a bunch of little ones this time. Think of a scene you want to make -- Grampa's home, for instance -- and all the things which make up that scene: the house, evergreen bushes, maple trees, mailbox, grampa, grandma, their dog, the garden, etc. Supply the children with white construction paper and crayons and read off the list of the items you need to make the scene. Let each child decide what part he or she wants to draw, and give them a little guidance on how large or small to make the object.

When all the drawings are finished they are cut out and assembled on a piece of posterboard. You will be amazed at how nice it will look because you can overlap the individual drawings to look more realistic (i.e. evergreen bushes on top of the front bottom edge of the house, large trees sticking out behind the house). Move the pieces around until everyone is in agreement on the arrangement, and then glue the cutouts to the posterboard. Add a brown construction paper frame and put the finished picture on display for everyone at the reunion to admire.

RETRIEVING COINS FROM STRAW

William Hundley of Oregon reports that a favorite activity for the children at Lilly Clan Reunions is hunting for games and coins which have been hidden in a loose bale of straw.

PAPER AIRPLANE CONTEST

This activity will appeal to children of a wide age range, is easy to set up, and requires no supervision. You supply scrap paper for making paper airplanes and hang a hulahoop from a tree limb or the ceiling. The children test their designing and flying skills by trying to fly their creations through the suspended hoop. You might want to also have some paper clips and scotch tape available for these aeronautical engineers.

WATER SLIDE

If you are holding the reunion outside on a hot, summer day and have an open grassy slope available consider making a water slide for the younger children. You will need a durable plastic sheet which is at least 15 feet long (look in do-it-yourself centers). Use old plastic milk jugs filled with water to hold the corners in place and turn a hose on at the top of the slide. The kids take a running leap and slide down the wet plastic; for safety sake make sure only one child slides down at a time. Be sure to inform parents in advance what you have planned so that they can bring swimsuits for the children.

PADDLEBALL OLYMPICS

Buy two or three inexpensive paddleballs and paint the name of the reunion, date, and place on the back of each paddle. Young and old can compete in a Family Paddleball Contest to see who can hit the ball with the paddle the most times in a row without missing. Give each person three tries and take the best score of the three. Have a posterboard or chalk board ready to record the names of the competitors and their scores. The winners get to take home the paddleballs as souvenirs.

MINI CAR RACES

Children love playing with mini cars (such as the Matchbox brand), so one family came up with the idea of setting up a double racetrack in their backyard for all the children at the gathering to enjoy. They browsed around the local home improvement store for something inexpensive to make tracks from and ended up buying three pieces of standard length gutter. Each piece was cut down the length to make six long pieces -- three for each track. The double track started on the balcony of an elevated play house and sloped down to the top of a stepladder. There, two more pieces of track were added by placing a scrap of plywood underneath each joint and fastening it securely with duct tape. The ends of the second lengths rested on a step halfway down a second stepladder, where the third sections were added. These ended on the ground. The children raced their cars most of the afternoon, leaving the adults free to watch from a distance and visit.

This is just one example of what you can make a track from. Take a mini car with you to a do-it-yourself center and use your imagination. Flat wood trim with quarter round attached along the edges would also work, as well as a number of other things. Take advantage of whatever is on sale. It doesn't take much of a slope for the cars to run, and the longer the track the better. Don't worry if there are bumps and sags in the track; as long as the car will still go down it, these make racing all the more fun!

Although this activity takes a little more time and equipment to set up than some of the other activities, the pleasure that the children get from it makes it all worthwhile. They can play for hours without an adult hovering over them. Young cousins (and even not-so-young cousins!) will end up organizing their own races and get to know each other better in the process. Be sure to tell the children in advance to bring mini cars to the reunion.

HIKES

Hikes are an activity that both children and adults can enjoy together. Children can find pretty rocks along the way to take home as a memento of the fun times they had with their cousins. Pretty flower blossoms and leaves can be collected to make a decoration to hang in a bedroom window at home. To do this, place the petals or leaves between two pieces of waxed paper and press with a hot iron; cut it into a circle or heart shape, punch a small hole at the top, and insert a piece of fishing line or invisible thread for hanging. A small circle of paper with the name and date of the reunion printed on it could be included between the waxed papers.

One type of hike that children often enjoy is a Penny Hike. The group takes ten steps forward and flips a penny. If the penny is 'heads' the group turns right and takes ten steps. If the penny is 'tails' the group turns left and takes ten steps. After every ten steps (or how many ever you decide on) the penny is flipped again. A variation is to divide into two groups with a penny for each group. Go to the center of an area (grassy area, room, etc.) and see which group will get out to the boundary (road, wall) first through the toss of the coin!

If you are holding your reunion in a park or forest preserve check in advance to see if there are any organized, informative nature hikes planned during the same time as your reunion. If the park rangers learn of your family's interest in participating in one, they may be willing to schedule a nature walk on the date you would like. If so, let them know whether the group will be primarily children or adults so that they can accommodate the understanding and interest level of that age group.

Ruth Bouma of Texas reports that when the Cooper family organized an early morning walking tour of the Calvin College campus (where the reunion was held) and nature preserve, a member of the biology department led the group and gave appropriate commentary on the sights along the way. What a great way to work up an appetite for breakfast!

The Elliott family has a tradition of an annual Saturday night hike. Everyone who wants to -- teenage and older -- takes a flashlight and goes for a walk through the woods. Where they go isn't important to the cousins; they just enjoy the cool night air, the exercise, and doing something as a group. Often older members of the family who don't want to go will volunteer to keep an eye on little children sleeping in the tents so that young parents can join their cousins for this tradition.

NAME SEARCH PUZZLE

Need a quiet activity for the children to do while the adults conduct a business meeting? Make your own name search puzzle using names of people in your family. Draw a grid of squares (1/4" to 1/2", depending on how large the letters will be) as shown in Fig. 91. Print the names of relatives in the squares, using block letters and going in any direction: up, down, forward, backward, and diagonally. Fill any squares still blank with random letters. Below the puzzle print a list of the names included in the puzzle so the children can mark off each one as they find it. Make plenty of copies.

Figure 91. Sample name search puzzle.

A	B	R	A	H	A	M	D	H	A	I	S	I	A
D	B	M	A	I	L	L	I	W	O	L	N	K	M
A	D	A	R	R	Z	R	A	I	E	I	U	O	D
L	S	L	T	A	O	C	N	L	L	S	N	Z	R
I	R	E	O	H	T	N	A	M	L	A	N	Q	O
N	A	U	J	R	S	A	A	A	G	S	A	G	E
E	C	M	C	N	E	H	Z	A	B	A	L	O	N
A	H	A	M	O	N	T	E	R	N	E	L	L	A
R	A	S	W	O	R	R	A	B	N	G	E	J	T
I	E	U	V	S	E	A	S	T	A	R	E	C	S
S	L	Y	E	R	M	M	M	F	H	R	Z	M	A
S	O	T	A	A	L	S	I	A	T	I	R	N	L
A	A	A	L	B	E	R	T	H	A	K	N	Y	I
C	Y	N	T	H	I	A	H	T	N	A	M	A	S

FAMILY FIRST NAMES

ABE	IRA
ABRAHAM	IRENE
ADA	ISIAH
ADELINE	ISSAC
ALBERT	MARTHA
ALLEN	NATHAN
ALMA	NOLA
ANNA	RACHAEL
ART	RITA
BARRY	RONA
BATHSHEBA	SAMANTHA
BERTHA	SAMUEL
CYNTHA	SILAS
ELMER	WILLIAM
ERNEST	WILMA
HIRA	ZULA

FAMILY SURNAMES

BARROWS
BARSON
BAYER
CATES
HAMLIN
OGLE
ORR
REAGAN
SMITH
STANFORD

SERIAL STORY

Here's a fun activity for children who are sitting around a campfire or in sleeping bags at night: one person starts telling story; it could be about a haunted house, a fictional caveman ancestor, or whatever he or she chooses. After two to five minutes another person takes up the tale and continues it for a while, and so on. Usually each person brings the character up to an impending disaster, scary event, or decision.

RHYMING REUNIONITES

Here's a good mixer game to break the ice: Think up enough pairs of rhyming words (age & page, cheer & near, etc.) so that you have a word for each person in the group. Print the words on separate slips of paper, put them in a box, and have each person draw one. Instruct everyone to find the person with a rhyming word and then create a poem together uses these two words (and additional rhyming words if they want). Each pair of rhyming reunionites recites their original poem to the rest of the group.

For a variation try four-person teams with sets of four rhyming words. Use a rhyming dictionary to help find some interesting sets of words -- the more unrelated the better!

FORM A KITCHEN BAND

A kitchen band can be hilarious as an activity by itself or as part of a talent show. Kitchens contain a wealth of possibilities for musical instruments! For instance, fill several drinking glasses with varying levels of water and you can tap out a tune on the rims with a spoon. Use two pan lids for cymbals. Tap together two wooden spoons for rhythm instruments, or use the bottom of a large kettle for a drum. Stretch some rubberbands over a meatloaf pan for a string instrument. Blow across the top of a jug. Tell everyone to look around and use their imaginations. You might want to have a contest between two bands for the title of Most Melodious; it could be adults versus children, aunts and uncles versus cousins, etc.

PHOTO CONCENTRATION GAME

Here is a game that will be popular at your family reunion for a variety of reasons: First, it is personalized because you use your own photographs to make it. Second, all different ages can play it -- making it good for mixing up the generations. Third, it is both easy and hard to play; there are very few rules to learn, and you can make it harder or easier according to how many pieces you play at one time. Two to four people can play at one time.

Decide what photos you want to use; these could be of past or present family members, homes owned by family members, pets, Grampa's fishing boat, etc. Take the photos to a print shop and have two color copies made of each photo. (Hint: tape as many photos as will fit on 8 1/2 x 11" sheets of paper since the print shop will be charging you by the sheet, not by the photograph.) Cut a 1 1/2" x 1 1/2" square from each color copy.

Next, cut 1/4" thick plywood into squares slightly larger than the photo squares; you will need one wood square for each photo. Glue a photo square to one side of each wood square. Use a woodburning tool or paint to write the family surname on the other side of each wood square. Finish the squares with two coats of clear polyurethane. Make 15 to 20 pairs of photo squares for the game, although you may not want to use the whole set when very young children are playing.

To play the game spread all the pieces out on a table, photo side down, and mix them around to make sure no one knows where any particular piece is. The first player turns over any two pieces. If the photos match he keeps the set and tries another two pieces. If the photos do not match he turns the photo sides down again and the person on his right tries. The person with the most matched sets wins.

Additional Suggestions:

You could also use corrugated cardboard or foam squares cut from meat trays instead of wood squares. The wood however (besides looking more attractive) has one advantage over cardboard or foam: when not playing the Photo Concentration Game children like to line them up in a row and watch them fall like dominoes, listening to the rhythmic clack-clack-clack sound of each piece falling against the next. Wood will also last longer.

Photo 33

If you are using photos of things or people who are not known to everyone you might want to make the wood squares large enough to write a line of identification below the picture. This could be a great way to acquaint a young person with what Great Great Grampa Wilson or his homesteading sod hut looked like.

A Photo Concentration Game would make a wonderful, unique door prize or auction item.

DECORATING COOKIE HOUSES

This is one of the most popular ideas for children you will ever come across, and we're talking tiny tots to teenagers! It is a particularly good activity for cousins with a big age range to do together.

Recipe for Cookie Dough:
 2 cups (4 sticks) butter or margarine
 2 cups sugar
 4 tablespoons milk
 2 teaspoons vanilla
 5 cups all-purpose flour

In a large bowl beat butter or margarine with electric mixer until softened. Add sugar and beat until fluffy. Add milk and vanilla. Beat well. Gradually mix in flour.

Divide dough into balls. Put in a plastic bag or clear plastic wrap and chill in refrigerator until firm -- one or two hours. Note: this recipe will make about seven houses, depending on how thin you roll out the dough. Any other recipe for cut-out cookies could also be substituted.

Photo 34: Cookie houses--fun to make and eat!

Recipe for Icing for Assembly:
Whites from 3 large eggs
1/2 tsp cream of tartar
1 pound confectioners' sugar

In a large bowl beat egg whites and cream of tartar with electric mixer until frothy. Gradually add confectioners' sugar and beat 5 to 7 minutes until thick and glossy. (Makes enough icing to assemble 15 to 20 houses)

Instructions:
1. Make cardboard patterns for the house pieces according to the dimensions shown in Fig. 92.

Figure 92. Cookie house patterns.

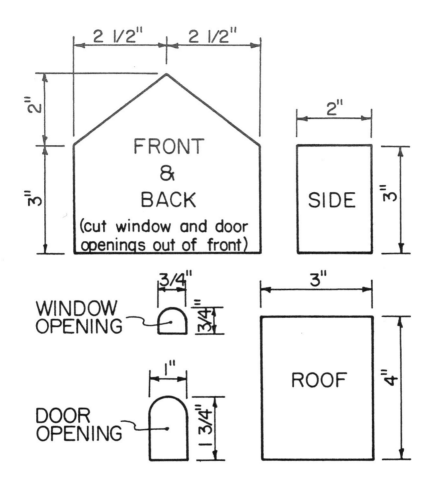

2. Make as many batches of the cookie dough as needed. Keep the balls of dough chilled until you are ready to roll each one out on a floured board. Place patterns on rolled out dough and use the tip of a knife to cut around each piece. Each house requires one front, one back, two sides, and two roof pieces. Hint: Cut out the fronts (without door and window openings) and place them on a cookie sheet; then position the door and window pattern on each front and carefully cut out the openings.

Bake on ungreased cookie sheets at 375 degrees for about 8 minutes or until edges just start to turn brown. Carefully remove pieces from baking sheet and let cool.

3. Cut 6" by 9" bases -- one for each cookie house -- from corrugated cardboard, and cover with colorful contact paper.

4. Assemble a cookie house on each base using the Icing for Assembly in a cake-decorating bag with a small tip.

Photo 35: Run a line of icing around the outside bottom
of each house to secure it to the base.

5. Now comes the fun part: decorating! Buy an assortment of small candies and place them in several bowls on the table so that everyone can share. Fill a decorating bag (with a small tip) with ready-made canned frosting; an adult or teenager is in charge of the icing and goes around the table squirting it wherever on the houses the children want it. (Suggestion: start by outlining one side of the roof on each house first. This can be done quickly and give everyone something to start working on. The next time around the table ask the child where he or she wants more frosting.) One 16 ounce can of frosting will be enough for about 12 houses.

The kids decide what kind of candy they want to use and where in the wet frosting to place it. Be sure to take pictures. You'll love the designs they come up with! You may want to suggest special touches such as a chimney (build up layers of frosting and candy), candy front steps, and gumdrop bushes.

Photo 36: One adult can handle five to seven children at one table.

UGLY FACE CONTEST

Who in your family can make the ugliest face? Hold a contest to find out! Take a self-developing snapshot of each contestant's effort and let everyone vote for the winner and runner-up. It's hilarious to watch and all ages can participate. Give each participant their own photo to take home and have a trophy or certificate for the winner.

CALLING COMPETITION

Adults and children can participate but it is best to have separate competitions for them. See who can most effectively or most loudly yell for cows, pigs, husbands, wives, or whatever.

T-SHIRT SLUMBER PARTY

Buy an extra large man's t-shirt for each young cousin and let them spend part of the morning decorating the shirts with tubes of fabric paint. By bedtime the shirts will be dry and can be used for comfy pajama tops for a slumber party. Insert a grocery sack or a piece of cardboard inside each shirt before painting so that the paint doesn't bleed through to the other side (but be sure to jiggle the sack every once in a while to make sure the paint isn't sticking to it). Print the name and year of the reunion somewhere on the t-shirt ahead of time.

WALNUT SHELL SAILBOATS

Figure 93. Walnut sailboat.

Have each child make a sailboat out of half of a walnut shell, toothpicks, a triangle cut from an index card, and glue as shown. Write names on the sails and try them out in a water-filled wading pool. The children will have fun huffing and puffing them to the other side of the pool.

BLOWING SOAP BUBBLES

When planning activities for young children, don't overlook the simple enjoyment of blowing bubbles. Individual bottles of solution and a blower can be purchased very inexpensively so that everyone has their own container. Suggestion: pour about a third of the solution from each bottle into a storage container to use for refills later. The children will be less likely to spill the solution on themselves when they are jumping around trying to catch the bubbles, and you will have extra solution for those who need a refill.

MAKING UP HISTORY

This activity is perfect for cousins sitting around a campfire in the evening. You need at least four people to make this fun; the more the merrier!

Give each person seven slips of paper and a pencil, and have them number the pieces of paper 1, 2, 3, 4, 5, 6, and 7. Tell them to think up a story about a male and female -- past or present -- in the family. They will write down the story on the slips of paper in the following format:

On paper #1 write his name.
On paper #2 write her name.
On paper #3 write where the two people are when the story takes place.
On paper #4 write what they are doing.
On paper #5 write what he said.
On paper #6 write what she said.
On paper #7 write what happened as a result of this.

When everyone has finished collect all the papers numbered 1 in one container, all papers numbered 2 in another container, and so on. Mix up the papers in each container and make another circle around the group. Each person takes one paper from each container and reads the final story to the group. The resulting stories can be hilarious. The reader can ad lib a bit to make the story read more smoothly, adding phrases such as "Once upon a time...", "Well, after he said that there was only one thing she could say:...", "unfortunately the result was that...". You might want to state a category of stories such as Famous Arguments in the Smith Family or Henderson Family Courtships.

PHOTOGRAPHY FUN

There is usually an abundance of cameras at reunions so why not create some extra photo-taking opportunities? Have everyone scavenge through attics and second-hand shops for old-fashioned clothing and accessories. Set up an area where children and adults dress in these outfits and be photographed individually or in groups. For extra fun, rig up a curtained 'stage' and have groups of two or more people take turns posing in humorous positions behind the curtain. They freeze their position for the opening of the curtain and the clicking of the cameras! After the group takes a bow the curtain is closed and another group takes their turn. You will end up with some very memorable photos! An emcee could ad-lib comments to describe the events leading up to the "...historic scene from our family's past which is about to be recreated before our very eyes." ("...Aunt Jane had seen the two rolling a cigarette behind the barn and had little sympathy for the current plight of their stomachs!")

Another idea is to purchase enough single-use cameras for every teenager present and challenge them to capture the essence of your family reunion on film. Teenagers are often dragged to reunions against their will; this might be just the thing to give them a whole new perspective on family gatherings. Have each person write his or her name on the camera before giving it back to you for developing so that you can keep track of who took which pictures. The best of the resulting photographs could be used in a special family newsletter or displayed at the next family reunion.

A Closer Look at Four Reunions

This chapter includes an in-depth look at four specific reunions: the National Odom Assembly, the Brauer-Crews Reunion, the Shelton-Fildes Reunion, and the Russell Reunion/Anniversary Celebration. Each one is distinctively different from the other three yet very representative of that type of reunion.

NATIONAL ODOM ASSEMBLY

The National Odom Assembly (NOA) is an example of a national organization which is based around a single surname: Odom. It is open to all descendants and researchers of this surname and currently has members in thirty-three American states, Australia, and Brazil. The group actively seeks others who might be interested in joining their organization.

The NOA bylaws (see end of this section) provide for an annual election of five officers: president, vice-president, secretary, treasurer, and editor. The president is elected from the state next in line to host the reunion, allowing him or her a year to plan and prepare for the event. (The President sets up any necessary committees to help accomplish this task, such as a Site Committee, Registration Committee, Hospitality Committee, Genealogy Committee, Banquet Committee, Entertainment Committee, etc.). The members of each state chapter also elect a state representative who, among other things, is the contact person in that state for anyone wishing to receive information about the NOA.

Annual dues for full membership in the organization are $20.00. Members are invited to the NOA annual get-together and receive the NOA News, a quarterly newsletter. The newsletter includes such items as: a report from each State Representative, open letters from other members, obituaries, wedding and birth announcements and other news, new genealogical information which has been uncovered, queries from NOA members and others about Odom ancestors, etc.

The annual reunions are held in a different state each year. The NOA members in the host state take great pride and care in planning an enjoyable and memorable get-together. In 1984 for example the location for the gathering was Augusta, Georgia. The planning committee met three times during the year before this event to present and discuss ideas, and make decisions. Representatives from the local tourist bureau, Chamber of Commerce, and the selected inn were present during these meetings to provide additional suggestions in their areas of expertise. Special committees were formed to handle Hospitality, Registration, Entertainment, and Genealogy details.

All of their planning paid off in a truly memorable gathering. The reunion officially began with registration at noon on Friday (and ended after a church service Sunday morning). Members had been encouraged to pre-register so that registration packets could be prepared ahead of time and be ready for them upon arrival. The contents of these packets vary each year, but include such items as name tags, printed schedule of events, banquet tickets, and commercial merchandise donated by different organizations, merchants, and individuals (pens, note pads, rulers, maps, thimbles, first-aid kits, tissues, matches, etc.). Sometimes the company that a NOA member works for will offer to provide free samples of their product; one of the Georgia NOA members was an executive for a candy company and a box of the candy was included in each registration packet that year.

Because many of the NOA members would be arriving for the reunion on Thursday evening, the planning committee set up a Hospitality Room in the hotel from 7:00 to 9:00 that evening. Bobbie Odom, Hospitality Chairman, enlisted the help of her two sisters and sister-in-law to prepare plenty of food for the Hospitality Room: cookies, cakes, brownies, candies, large bowls of fresh peaches sitting in crushed ice, carved watermelons filled with fruit, dips, sandwiches, and cheeseballs, plus gallons of coffee, punch, iced tea, and cokes. The hospitality room was also open for two hours on Friday afternoon and two hours on Saturday afternoon.

One suggestion of the NOA president that year, Frank Odom, was that each State Representative be asked to bring a flag of their state with them to the reunion. These made a colorful display behind the table reserved specifically for State representatives. The opening of the Friday evening meeting included welcome speeches from the mayor of Augusta (who also proclaimed a specific day 'Odom Day'), the chairman of the county board of commissioners, and the reigning Miss Augusta. After receiving a letter from the NOA president about the upcoming reunion, President and Nancy

Reagan had written a letter to the NOA; this occasion was used to present the letter to the membership. Also, the governor of Georgia made every NOA State Representative a Lieutenant Colonel, Aide De Camp, Governor's Staff, and these recognitions were presented during the program. Because that year was the fifth anniversary of the formation of the NOA, the host group decided to award an attendance pin to each person who had attended all five reunions.

Photo 37: Courtesy of Dorothy Odom Bruce. The NOA president leads the group in singing the Odom ballad. The flower arrangement on the table is in memory of all NOA members who have died during the last year."

On Saturday morning the Augusta Chamber of Commerce arranged to have as many buses as needed to take NOA guests on a free two-hour historical tour of Augusta, with tour guides for each bus. After the tour free time was scheduled to allow attendees the opportunity to pursue their own interests and visit with old friends and new acquaintances. Many people who have been in charge of organizing a reunion have emphasized the need to 'schedule' a block of time for this purpose.

A buffet banquet dinner was held Saturday evening, and the hours of planning and work which went into the details of it again paid off. Bobbie Odom and her brother made special table decorations for the occasion: "We gathered tree limbs from the woods with fungi on them and he cut them in 1' sections and bored holes at intervals in them for silk flowers and leaves," says Bobbie. "I glued butterflies to a large toothpick and had them flying just above the flowers. The flowers were yellow and white, the motif I worked with, and I put three on each table. These were given later as door prizes to those who had a number under their chairs at each table that corresponded with the ones under the limb."

A variety of other door prizes were given away throughout the evening: portable hair dryers, radios, sets of bowls, garden tools, children's games, linens, etc. which were donated by local merchants. Bobbie also arranged for other games during the banquet which gave even more people an opportunity to take home a beautifully wrapped prize: "One of the games was that I had a list of things and called them one at a time at different parts of the banquet room," says Bobbie. "They were like 'the first one who gets to me who has a fingernail file in their purse' or 'the first man who has shoes on that do not lace up'. You would be amazed to see the participation in such a game and no matter the age of the participants!"

Photo 38: Courtesy of Dorothy Odom Bruce. Bobbie uses a microphone to make sure everyone can hear during the evening's games and presentation of door prizes.

One person who picked up the napkin at his place setting at the table found a card Bobbie had placed there in advance. It read, "If you will wait until after dinner, get to your feet and get everybody's attention, and tell who you are and where you are from you will receive a gift."

"I did not know John Denny of Tulsa before that night but he was the one who got this napkin and he was wonderful," says Bobbie. "He made it so special and made up lots of stuff about the lady in front of him and had everyone howling with laughter, and later I learned this was his wife."

All of these details and careful attention to planning make the NOA gatherings spectacularly successful. Naturally each state group, when taking a turn as host, wants to uphold the level of hospitality and fun shown by previous groups. The NOA has also undertaken other special projects, such as the NOA Cookbook published in 1989 for the tenth anniversary of the organization. Along with favorite recipes, the book includes a history of how the organization began and the words and music for the copyrighted Odom Ballad. One line in the ballad states a very obvious fact about this group: "...We're Odoms in America, we're proud of our name."

NATIONAL ODOM ASSEMBLY CONSTITUTION

PREAMBLE: This constitution was adopted at the fourth Annual Meeting of the National Odom Assembly in Austin, TX on July 23, 1983.

I. NAME: The name of the organization shall be THE NATIONAL ODOM ASSEMBLY.

II. PURPOSE: The purpose and objectives of the organization shall be:
   (a) Encourage genealogical research on all branches of the greater ODOM family and the sharing of that research; and
   (b) Promote fun and fellowship among its members.

III. MEMBERSHIP: Membership in NOA shall be on a yearly basis and shall be effective upon the payment of annual dues. The NOA membership shall begin July 1 and end June 30.

Membership in the NOA shall be composed of Odom descendants and other interested Odom researchers, with the following categories of membership:

(a) FULL MEMBER shall have voting privileges, be eligible to hold office in the NOA, be exempt from registration fees at the annual meetings, and receive the quarterly newsletter.

(b) ASSOCIATE MEMBER shall receive the quarterly newsletter and be permitted to place inquiries in the newsletter. The associate membership fee shall be one-half the cost of full membership.

Membership fees shall be set by the Executive Board.

Photo 39: Courtesy of Dorothy Odom Bruce. When the gathering was held in Texas, small Texas flags were given to the children as they told the audience their name and what state they were from.

IV. OFFICERS: The officers of the NOA shall consist of a president, vice-president, secretary, treasurer, and editor.

(a) The duties of a president shall be to preside at the annual meeting and be responsible for the general affairs of the NOA during his or her term of office.

(b) The duties of the vice president shall be to preside in the absence of the president and to serve in the capacity as president when called upon to do so in the absence of the president, and generally assist in all affairs of the NOA.

(c) The duties of the secretary shall be to record the minutes and be responsible for caring for the general correspondence of the NOA.

(d) The duties of the treasurer shall be to receive and disburse the funds of the NOA pursuant to general direction issued by the Executive Board.

(e) The duties of the editor shall be to prepare and mail to members a quarterly newsletter.

All officers shall serve for a term of one year or until a successor is elected; all officers are eligible for re-election.

Photo 40: Courtesy of Dorothy Odom Bruce. A group photo is taken of all officers and state representatives present."

V. EXECUTIVE BOARD: The officers of the NOA and the immediate past president shall constitute the Executive Board. The officers of the NOA shall be the officers of the Executive Board.

The Executive Board shall have general supervision of the affairs of the organization between general membership meetings. It is subject to the orders of the NOA, and none of its action shall conflict with the action taken by the organization at any membership meeting.

The Executive Board shall have the power to replace officers who resign, become inactive, or die during their term of office.

VI. COMMITTEES: Committees of the NOA shall consist of the following:

(a) A PROGRAM COMMITTEE composed of the president and vice president along with other members who may be appointed by the president to plan the program for the upcoming annual meeting, or such other meeting of the general membership as may be duly called.

(b) A HOSPITALITY COMMITTEE shall be appointed by the president and shall secure a suitable location for the annual meeting, and notify members no later than January 1st of the year in which the annual meeting shall be held.

(c) A NOMINATING COMMITTEE shall be composed of at least three state representatives in attendance at the annual meeting, and such others as the president may appoint, who shall present a slate of officers after ascertaining the willingness of each person to serve. Additional nominations may also be made from the floor, provided the same condition of a candidate's willingness to serve has been met.

(d) Such other committees or chairmen of committees, as shall be appointed by the president of NOA.

VII. PUBLICATION: The organization will publish a newsletter to be published and mailed quarterly and which shall be known as NOA NEWS. It shall be published quarterly and mailed in January, April, July, and October.

VIII. PARLIAMENTARY AUTHORITY: The rules contained in the most current issues of Robert's Rules of Order, newly revised, shall govern the organization in all cases to which they are applicable.

IX. AMENDMENTS: These bylaws may be amended at any regular business meeting of the organization by a two-thirds vote, provided the proposed amendment has been submitted in writing at the previous regular business session of a general meeting. Unless otherwise provided, prior to its adoption or in the motion to adopt, an amendment shall become effective upon adjournment of the annual meeting at which it is adopted.

BRAUER-CREWS REUNION

The Brauer-Crews Reunion is an example of a week-long, multi-generation gathering which uses committees and meets at a non-home location. The two families became connected in the 1880s when two Brauer brothers married two Crews sisters. The twelve siblings/double cousins that resulted from these two marriages felt an especially close kinship with each other. Years later when this second generation had scattered to establish their own households one person suggested a joint vacation/reunion so that their children, the third generation, could have an opportunity to get acquainted and celebrate their special ancestry. This event has become a tradition called the Brauer-Crews Reunion.

These family gatherings take place during the third week in June. Originally they were scheduled for every five years, but after a few reunions this was shortened to every three years and finally to every other year. These very successful joint vacations/reunions continue, giving everyone a chance to catch up what is happening in each other's lives, remember the past, and celebrate the future.

Initially there was a different host family each year in charge of reunion details such as deciding on a theme, planning the activities, etc. The chosen theme was carried out with appropriate decorations and entertainment. A Hawaiian theme included dressing in Island wear and having a luau around the pool on theme night. For a Western theme everyone dressed in Western wear for the theme night; the children of the host family put on a square dance demonstration and afterwards everyone was encouraged to join in on the fun of a Western hoedown.

The group eventually switched to using a committee for planning the reunions. The committee in charge of the next reunion holds its first planning session during the current reunion. They meet again during the fall season preceding next reunion, and the third planning meeting is held in January or February.

The group prefers to meet in scenic nature areas, such as the Sequoia National Park, where there are plenty of opportunities for hiking, swimming, campfires, etc. The families stay in cabins, RVs or campsites -- as close as possible to each other. One of the years that the group met in Gurneville, two side-by-side resorts were used to accommodate the 100 to 130 family members who attended.

Old favorites and new ideas are incorporated into a list of planned activities for the week. Traditionally from 9 to 10 o'clock each morning a couple of the young mothers hold an arts and crafts session for all of the children. It's a fun-filled time of learning songs, drawing pictures, painting rocks, making clay figures, collecting pine cones, or whatever -- a great way to nurture family ties among the youngest members of the clan. An added bonus is that while the children are busy, their parents are free to pursue their own interests: relaxing quietly, visiting, or attending band practice.

The band is another Brauer-Crews Reunion tradition. Because so many family members through the years have played musical instruments, taught music, and organized school bands, it was natural for them to put their talents to use for the entertainment of the group. The band practices for one hour each morning, and is open to anyone in the family who would like to join the fun. They perform for the rest of the group on Saturday evening during another tradition -- the family talent show.

This talent show always includes a variety of acts: skits, dances, singing, dog acts, Uncle Easton's Magic Show, tumbling demonstrations, poets reading something they have written, dramatic interpretation, etc. Some of these have been planned and practiced well in advance; others are spur-of-the-moment creations. A touch of humor here and there is always appreciated; one year when a triple trio (nine singing women) were getting ready to perform, the emcee introduced them as a new singing group who for the first time was appearing on records. When the singers got to the front of the room they each laid a record album jacket on the floor and stood on it!

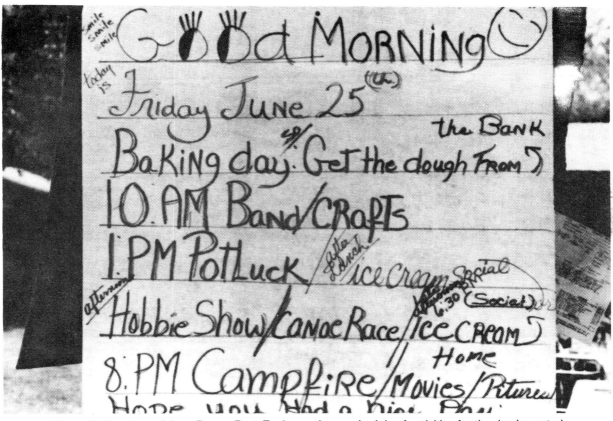

Photo 41: Courtesy of Jean Brauer Burt. Each morning a schedule of activities for the day is posted.

Photo 42: Courtesy of Jean Brauer Burt. The family band holds their practice outdoors.

Photo 43: Courtesy of Jean Brauer Burt. Two young girls entertain the rest of the family with a song.

Performances by the children in the family are always a big hit. One year they marched in playing rhythm band instruments to the beat of a drum. They lined up at the front of the room and one little girl stood in front and directed them in a short song with gestures. The adult family band played "Whistle While You Work" and the children joined in with their rhythm instruments. The children then marched back out, keeping their performance appropriately short and simple.

Photo 44: "Courtesy of Jean Brauer Burt. Talent show performances by the youngest generation are always especially enjoyable.

One year a cousin performed a pantomime act that was a real show stopper:

"When they announced Cousin Albert, he proceeded to get up and do a pantomime of what he sees his wife do to put on her makeup every morning," relates Patricia Ray. "The kids were simply mesmerized with his antics and everyone was laughing. His wife was laughing so hard she cried."

Another old favorite on the Brauer-Crews reunion agenda is the hobby show on Saturday afternoon. It's a wonderful opportunity to see what the family artists, inventors, authors, collectors, and craftsmen have been up to since the last reunion. The arts and crafts that the children have been working on all week are also displayed. Sometimes a hall is rented to use for both the hobby show and the talent show; the resort where one reunion was held graciously supplied a big tent for these types of activities.

On one evening during the week the family holds an auction to help raise money for the Reunion Planning Fund. Everyone donates something; it could be a beautiful piece of needlework or original poetry by a family poet. Someone in the family volunteers to be the auctioneer and the bidding begins. The family has also raised money for the Fund by setting up a snack stand at one of their evening programs.

Past family history is kept alive through stories told around evening campfires and special programs. One member of the older generation often put together interesting slide shows:

"1974 was the last time that Leo showed his slides of ancestors and told the stories that went with the pictures," says Jean Brauer-Burt. "I had a new tape recorder and placed it next to him as he talked. I captured his words on tape and when all of his pictures, negatives, and photo equipment were given to me after his death it gave me the material to make a video of the pictures with him narrating his story."

Jean has also made recordings of other family members:

"In 1984 I had a video camera and had the inspiration to get people to sit down and talk about their life. I asked 96-year-old Leslie to sit down and talk with me. He told me many stories of their life in Shasta County and sang many of the songs he had learned as a child. What a treasure!"

One year the group included a genealogy workshop in the week's agenda for the benefit of those who were just starting to do genealogy. During another reunion they sent letters which had been signed by everyone present to those family members who hadn't been able to attend, letting them know that they were being thought of and missed. Whenever there has been a death in the family since the last gathering, a short memorial story about the person's life is read aloud sometime during the week.

During the week softball games, volleyball games, field trips to local points of interest, hikes, and sing-alongs are organized. Lazy afternoons of swimming and visiting are followed by evenings of roasting marshmallows and story telling. Many family members are Seventh Day Adventists, so on Saturday they hold a church service or attend one in the nearest town. Group pictures are taken that afternoon while everyone is still dressed up.

Photo 45: Courtesy of Jean Brauer Burt. A special reunion treat -- homemade strawberry ice cream.

The week spent together enjoying nature and each other renews the family spirit and strengthens the kinship bond. One year a mother and daughter wrote the following song which exemplifies the pride this group takes in their reunions:

BRAUER-CREWS REUNION THEME SONG
by
Margaret Hill and Vivian Reiswig
(sing to the tune of The Battle Hymn of the Republic)

Mine eyes have seen the wonder
Of the gathering of the clan
As they come from o'er the nation
In an ever widening span.
Tho they had a small beginning
They have spread across the land,
As time goes marching on.

Chorus:
Long live the reunion
Long live the reunion
Long live the reunion
As time goes marching on.

In the beauty of the forest
Where all nature strives to please.
We have gathered 'neath the redwoods
Blending voices on the breeze.

As we build enduring friendships
Everlasting as the trees,
As time goes marching on.

(Chorus)

Our reunion now has ended
We must go our separate ways,
But the memory will linger
Through the intervening days
So until the next reunion
Let us all our voices raise
As time goes marching on

(Chorus)

SHELTON-FILDES REUNION

The Shelton-Fildes Reunion is another example of a multi-generation reunion, but unlike the Brauer-Crews Reunion it is held at a private home and does not use committees. During the second weekend in June Bob and Helen Walker host a two-day Shelton-Fildes Reunion at their home in southern Illinois, a Christmas tree farm near the small town of Cisne. This land has been in the family since 1868 and is centrally located for the one hundred or so relatives and family friends who attend the annual gathering. There is ample space in the large shaded yard for tents and campers, and a well-stocked pond is available for those who would like to mix a little fishing with the weekend of visiting.

Since the reunion is held on the same weekend each year it is easy for relatives to know which weekend to keep open. Notices about the yearly gathering are included in the genealogy books Helen has published for several branches of the family. She also includes reminders about it in Christmas cards and puts a notice in the local newspaper a week or two before the reunion weekend. Newly discovered relatives receive a special mailing:

"I send additional information to 'new' relatives who plan to attend such as how to find this farm, motels in the area or bed reservations here or with one of my sisters who lives near here, tentative agenda for the weekend, names of others they really want to meet or see again," says Helen. Everyone is encouraged to bring along family friends, fishing poles, games, food to share, lawn chairs, sleeping bags, tents, cameras, insect repellent, old photos and photo albums to share, etc.

The family has no official committees to tend to the preliminary work for each reunion; Helen prefers to handle this herself. As the day of the reunion approaches, however, plenty of family members volunteer to help with whatever needs to be done: mowing the lawn, setting up tables, stringing lights, hanging the reunion sign, gathering firewood for campfires, driving into town for groceries, preparing food, making name tags, setting up volleyball or croquet areas, etc.

"Some come a week early and they help in the preparations. Some stay a week after and they get to help in the cleanup," says Helen. "Saturday, everyone who came early becomes a host or hostess, as well as my children, my sisters, and my closest nieces and nephews." They greet and introduce all who arrive, have everyone sign the register and farm guest book, answer the telephone, help new arrivals with special needs, ice down drinks, play with the little ones in sandbox, take group and candid photos, and give tours of the farm, nearby cemeteries, and old homesites.

Photo 46: A father and son head down the lane to participate in one of the favorite reunion activities -- fishing at the farm pond.

Photo 47: Host Bob Walker catches on film the big one that didn't get away.

At noon on Saturday everyone contributes dishes of delicious home-cooked food for a shared dinner in the spacious back yard. There is often fresh farm produce to add to the table, and Helen personally makes sure there is enough of one family favorite: blackberry cobbler.

The afternoon is spent enjoying each other's company, catching up on old times and new happenings, playing games, and fishing in this quiet rural setting. When the sound of car tires on gravel is heard all eyes turn toward the driveway to see who the latest arrival is. The person or family is warmly greeted with "You made it!", followed by hugs and any introductions that might be needed.

A large campfire is lit early Saturday evening in order to allow it to burn down just the right amount for roasting hot dogs for supper. Many people who aren't able to attend during the day because of work or other commitments arrive in the evening for the wiener roast and cookout. It is during these quiet, comfortable evenings, while gentle breezes rustle the tree leaves and bob-whites call from the woods, that the younger generation -- almost by osmosis -- begins to absorb into their memories the family stories told by the older generations: stories about Grandma Shelton's house being moved with a single horse, the infamous Shelton gang, and childhood pranks. It will be this generation, and these reunions, which will keep these stories alive for future generations of the family to enjoy.

Photo 48: Pitting cherries becomes an enjoyable afternoon task when combined with plenty of visiting around the dining table.

Photo 49: Saturday evening wiener roasts are a popular activity at many reunions, including this one.

On Sunday morning the Walkers prepare coffee and breakfast for everyone who stayed over-night, and those who wish to attend nearby churches. The noon meal on Sunday -- another back-yard basket dinner -- usually draws the largest crowd of the weekend. Afterwards Helen gives a welcoming speech, makes any necessary introductions, and often tells a little family history. The rest of the day is left open for visiting, games, and sharing before those who must leave for home begin saying their good-byes.

RUSSELL REUNION/ANNIVERSARY CELEBRATION

The Russell Reunion is an example of a small family reunion/joint vacation held at a non-home location. Charlotte and Fred Russell, Sr., of Michigan, their three sons, two daughters-in-law, and four grandchildren have enjoyed several of these combined reunions/vacations:

Photo 50: Courtesy of Jean Russell. The three generations of the Russell family.

"It gives everyone neutral time together on neutral turf," says daughter-in-law Jean Russell. "At our homes we are more confined and someone is always the host. Also, the children have other friends and activities going on. When on vacation we are only there to enjoy each other and to relax."

One very special and memorable reunion was held in April of 1990 when Charlotte and Fred -- in lieu of giving themselves an anniversary party -- paid the airfare and lodging expenses to take the entire family to Puerto Vallarta, Mexico. Charlotte worked with a travel agent to find a good location for reunion/anniversary celebration, looking for something suitable for the young grand-children (ages 1 1/2 years to 7 1/2 years) as well as the adults. They settled on Villa Pacifico (P.O. Box 198-B, La Marina at Beachfront, Jalisco, Puerto Vallarta, Mexico 48380). Each villa had two large bedrooms, kitchen, living/dining room, patio, and a view of the ocean.

"They were on the ground floor which made it nice when going to the beach or pool," says Jean. "and right next to each other down our own little hall so they were ideal to go back and forth be-tween them."

The family had done a lot of reading before the trip "...to get a feel for the area", and when they arrived at the villa the manager suggested several places the group might like to explore.

"After we settled in we talked about what we'd like to do -- golf, shopping, restaurants, tours, etc.," says Jean. "We also tried to discuss meal planning, nap needs for the little ones, grocery shopping, etc. We felt it best to take care of the logistics of the week and be sure everyone fit in what they wanted to do."

High on the list of things to do was simply relaxing and enjoying each other's company at the beach and pool. They ate breakfast and lunch in the villas, using food brought from home and food from a local grocery store, and went out for dinners. Some of the group outings were a day boat trip to a special beach you could only get to by boat (with silky sand, beautiful scenery, and dolphins), parasailing, an evening at a great Mexican fiesta, and a bus tour of the area which ended up at Chin's: "This was a lovely restaurant deep in the jungle surrounded by waterfalls," says Jean. "The best part was swimming in the waterfalls while we waited for our food to come."

Photo 51: Courtesy of Jean Russell. Fred Sr. enjoys an opportunity to try out parasailing during the week.

Separate outings were also planned so that each individual family had time to go out alone. One night Charlotte and Fred volunteered to watch their grandchildren so that the middle generation could go out together for dinner and dancing.

"It is hard to say what we all liked the most," says Jean. "We all get along well and probably enjoyed just being together. When traveling we have few demands -- no laundry, no phone calls, no deadlines, etc. Even when preparing a meal or cleaning up afterwards we did it all together so it was just fun."

Jean advises other families who might like to try this type of combined family vacation/reunion to do a lot of pre-planning. Decide in advance how to handle food, costs, etc. Agree that not everyone has to do everything together; plan something separate for each family unit to enjoy alone. Take time the first or second day to discuss everyone's expectations/needs/desires, and try to sketch out a basic outline of how the week will go.

"It helps to break off a bit," says Jean. "Let grandmother, Fred Jr., and Courtney go for a walk for example, or have Grampa, Fred Jr., Chuck, Drew, and Courtney go golfing. This gives people time apart, but also gives everyone special time together. You want to be sure everyone has time to really talk to each other and form some new memories."

State Tourism Offices

The packets of information sent out by state tourism offices can be very useful in locating state parks and other sites appropriate for family reunions. Write or call for a free tourist packet from the appropriate state.

Bureau of Tourism and Travel
532 S. Perry Street
Montgomery, AL 36104
(205) 242-4169
(800) 252-2262

Division of Tourism
Commerce and Economic Development Dept.
P.O. Box E
Juneau, AK 99811
(907) 465-2010

Office of Tourism
1100 W. Washington
Phoenix, AZ 85007
(602) 542-8687

Tourism Division
Department of Parks and Tourism
One Capitol Mall
Little Rock, AR 72201
(501) 682-7777
(800) 643-8383

Office of Tourism
801 K Street
Ste. 1600
Sacramento, CA 95814
(916) 322-2881
(800) 862-2543

Colorado Tourism Board
Department of Local Affairs
1625 Broadway
Room 1700
Denver, CO 80202
(303) 592-5410
(800) 265-6723

Tourism Division
Department of Economic Development
865 Brook Street
Rocky Hill, CT 06067
(203) 258-4286
(800) 282-6863

Committee to Promote Washington
415 12th Street, NW
Ste. 312
Washington, DC 20004
(202) 724-4091

Tourism Office
99 Kings Highway
P.O. Box 1401
Dover, DE 19901
(302) 736-4271
(800) 441-8846

Division of Tourism
Department of Commerce
505 Collins Building
107 W. Gaines Street
Tallahassee, FL 32399
(904) 488-5607

Tourist Division
Industry, Trade, and Tourism
285 Peachtree Ctr Ave., #1000
Atlanta, GA 30303
(404) 656-3553

Department of Business, Economic
   Development, & Tourism
220 S. King Street, #1100
Honolulu, HI 96813
(808) 548-6914

Tourism Development
Department of Commerce
700 W. State Street
Boise, ID 83720
(208) 334-2470
(800) 635-7820

Department of Commerce & Community Affairs
620 E. Adams Street
3rd Floor
Springfield, IL 62701
(217) 785-1032
(800) 223-0121

Tourism Development
Department of Commerce
1 N. Capitol
Indianapolis, IN 46204
    (317) 232-8870
    (800) 289-6646

Bureau of Tourism and Visitors
Department of Economic Development
200 E. Grand
Des Moines, IA 50309
    (515) 281-3401

Division of Travel and Tourism
Department of Commerce
400 SW Eighth
5th Floor
Topeka, KS 66603
    (913) 296-7091

Tourism Cabinet
Capitol Plaza Tower
Frankfort, KY 40601
    (502) 564-4270
    (800) 225-8747

Louisiana Office of Tourism
Culture, Recreation, and Tourism Department
P.O. Box 94291
Baton Rouge, LA 70804
    (504) 925-3850
    (800) 334-8626

Division of Tourism
Department of Economic and Community
    Development
State House Station #59
Augusta, ME 04333
    (207) 289-2656
    (800) 533-9595

Office of Tourism and Promotion
Department of Economic and Employment
    Development
217 E. Redwood St.
Baltimore, MD 21201
    (301) 333-6611
    (800) 543-1036

Division of Tourism
Department of Commerce and Development
100 Cambridge St., 13th Floor
Boston, MA 02202
    (617) 727-3205

Travel Bureau
Department of Commerce
P.O. Box 30226
Lansing, MI 48909
    (517) 373-0670
    (800) 543-2937

Office of Tourism
Farm Ctr Building
Room 250
375 Jackson Street
St. Paul, MN 55101
    (612) 296-2755
    (800) 657-3700

Division of Tourism
Department of Economic and Community
    Development
P.O. Box 849
Jackson, MS 39205
    (601) 359-3297
    (800) 647-2290

Division of Tourism
Department of Economic Development
Truman Building, Box 1055
Jefferson City, MO 65102
    (314) 751-3051

Montana Promotion Bureau
Department of Commerce
1424 Ninth Avenue
Helena, MT 59620
    (406) 444-2654
    (800) 541-1447

Division of Travel and Tourism
Department of Economic Development
P.O. Box 94666
Lincoln, NE 68509
    (402) 471-3111
    (800) 228-4307

Commission on Tourism
5151 S. Carson Street
Carson City, NV 89710
    (702) 687-4322
    (800) 638-2328

Vacation Travel Promotion Office
Resources and Economic Development Dept.
172 Pembroke Road
Concord, NH 03301
    (603) 271-2665

Division of Travel and Tourism
Commerce and Economic Development Dept.
20 W. State Street, CN826
Trenton, NJ 08625
   (609) 292-2470

Tourism Division
1100 St. Francis Dr.
Santa Fe, NM 87503
   (505) 827-0291
   (800) 545-2040

Department of Commerce
1 Commerce Plaza
Albany, NY 12245
   (518) 474-4100
   (800) 225-5697

Travel Development Division
Department of Economic and Community
  Development
430 N. Salisbury St.
Raleigh, NC 27603
   (919) 733-4171
   (800) 847-4862

Director of Tourism
Parks and Tourism Department
604 E. Blvd.
Bismarck, ND 58505
   (701) 224-2525
   (800) 437-2077

Office of Travel and Tourism
Department of Development
30 E. Broad Street.
25th Floor
Columbus, OH 43266
   (614) 466-8844
   (800) 282-5393

Tourism and Recreation Department
500 Will Rogers Building
Oklahoma City, OK 73105
   (405) 521-2413
   (800) 652-6552

Tourism Division
Department of Economic Development
775 Summer Street
Salem, OR 97310
   (503) 373-1230
   (800) 547-7842

Department of Commerce
433 Forum Building
Harrisburg, PA 17120
   (717) 783-3840
   (800) 847-4872

Director of Tourism
Department of Economic Development
7 Jackson Walkway
Providence, R.I. 02903
   (401) 277-2601
   (800) 556-2484

Division of Tourism
Parks, Recreation, and Tourism
1205 Pendleton Street
Columbia, SC 29201
   (803) 734-0135
   (800) 872-3505

Department of Tourism
Capitol Lake Plaza
Pierre, SD 57501
   (605) 773-3301
   (800) 843-1930

Department of Tourist Development
320 Sixth Avenue, N.
Nashville, TN 37243
   (615) 741-1904

Texas Department of Commerce
P.O. Box 12728
Austin, TX 78711
   (512) 472-5059
   (800) 888-8839

Division of Travel Development
Community & Economic Development Dept.
Council Hall and Capitol Hill
Salt Lake City, UT 84114
   (801) 538-1030

Travel Division
Agency of Development and Community Affairs
134 State Street
Montpelier, VT 05602
   (802) 828-3236

Division of Tourism
Department of Economic Development
1021 E. Cary Street
Richmond, VA 23219
   (804) 786-2051
   (800) 248-4833

Tourism Development Division
Trade and Economic Development Department
101 General Administration Building
M/S: AX-13
Olympia, WA 98504
   (206) 753-5795
   (800) 544-1800

Tourism Marketing Division
Division of Commerce
State Capitol Complex
Building 6
Charleston, WV 25305
   (304) 348-2286
   (800) 225-5982

Division of Tourism Development
Department of Development
P.O. Box 7970
Madison, WI 53707
   (608) 266-2147
   (800) 432-8747

Tourism Division
Department of Commerce
I-25 at College Drive
Cheyenne, WY 82002
   (307) 777-7777
   (800) 225-5996